Inspirational Poetry

By

Southern Chicks

Inspirational Poetry

By

Southern Chicks

Beverly S. Harless

Carol J. Hagan

Dedications

There are so many people that I would like to thank and dedicate my portion of this poetry book to. So many have encouraged me to continue writing poetry from the very first poem I penned.

There are a few people that I want to mention by name that have supported and cheered me on to do this project - my husband Jeff; my pastor and friend, Frankie Carroll; my daughter, Alison; and my co-worker and friend, Carol J. Hagan.

Thanks to everyone who has been a part of cheering my writing on.

- Beverly S. Harless

I'd like to dedicate my portion of this book to my parents, Bernice and Tommy Hagan.

I write about God, family, friends and just plain ole everyday life. My mother has severe Alzheimer's, and the toll it takes on a family going through this, often at times, seems to be unbearable. My Dad's a preacher and has been the role model that my family and even strangers strive to be like. Both of my parents have always been the type of people everybody wants to be like, but rarely ever are.

- Carol J. Hagan

Ever Learning

Sorrow and heartache do much abound,
Especially when it comes to family letting you down.
Disappointment and hurt are the most horrible things,
When it comes from loved ones being hurtful and mean.

Anger can mount and tears do flow,
Having been through this before - there is some things that I know:

Forgiveness is one of the most wonderful tools.
It brings peace and comfort to whom has been confronted with
arguments and deceitful rules.
Doing what's right in spite of harmful actions toward you,
Leaves you without regret and to the fire - doesn't fuel.

It takes pointing fingers and tongues full of accusing blame,
Without a target to aim at - putting those whom have done this to
more than just shame.
It keeps heads held high and eyes able to look straight at the truth,
Even when others are bending and twisting truth in attempt to
elude.

We will all have our share of such horrible things,
Ever learning how we should rightly handle feelings they bring.
We all have an example to follow in always doing what's right.
God gave us His Word to follow His Light - and also His Son -
Our Lord, Jesus Christ.

- Beverly S. Harless

When You Wanna Give Up

When you wanna give up on it all and deep inside you'd like to quit;
When you feel as if your life is totally in the pits;
When you feel as if no hope could possibly be in the cards;
Just step out on faith - life wasn't meant to be so hard.

When you feel as if your life is simply going nowhere
And you can't think of a soul in the world that you think cares;
When everything you touch seems to fall slam apart
And you feel like a dagger is constantly piercing your heart.

When you feel like you can't put one foot in front of the other;
When you opt to hide all pain thinking it's impossible to recover;
When depression starts consuming every inch of your life,
No one knowing your troubles since you wear that great disguise.

Someone that I know will be your trusted friend.
He will never forsake you - even there way past the end.
So when you feel like giving up, quitting and walking away,
Ask God to help you - this is the prayer I always pray.

- Carol J.Hagan

Long Before They've Passed On

All have lost someone they have loved.
When we do, we cling to the memory of their smiles and hugs.
Holding on so desperately to the smallest of things;
Their laughter, their giggles, or the way they did sing.
All of us living know it's a part of life's plan.
Everyone's time slips away - as sand we try to hold in our hand.
We grieve and mourn wanting back what we once had -
Forgetting a part of this world's life that is even more sad.

Arguments and feeling rise, from something so small.
We stand in anger - forgetting anyone else at all.
Commitments and promises are no longer our concern.
We turn to selfishness and resentment - we say things that burn.
We turn our backs on those who have loved us the most -
Those who have helped us with compassion - their kind deeds
elude us as ghosts.
Some shared their homes when we had nowhere to go,
And sacrificed for months or years putting first what you needed -
so easy to now tell them, "No".

All of this from forgetting where we were just a little while ago.
Everything others have done, away it is easy for us to throw.
It's sad how once we've come out of our need for help -
How we are no longer humble, even a parent or sister is no longer
important - only ourself.
There is no mourning or tears that are cried.
Only self righteous indigination, no willingness to try.
Family and friends so easily tossed to the side.
We could care less if we even say, "good-bye".

- Beverly S. Harless

Unanswered Prayers

Have you ever prayed and prayed everyday and every night,
For God to answer a prayer - no matter if the outcome was right?
For example you wanted another to be a part of your life,
But three years later on, you're now happy with your wife.

Have you ever prayed for a different job and you just couldn't see,
Years down the road you're still there but, the president of that company?
Have you ever prayed for another house but, the price you couldn't afford,
Ten years later with the deed in your hand, plus you own several more?

Have you ever prayed for a newer car and wondered why your request was stalled,
Two years later on the news, millions of that car were recalled?
Have you ever questioned God as why the traffic seems turtle slow,
Yet had you been rolling along you'd wrecked two miles up the road?

Have you ever begged for God to please spare someone's life?
They now reside with Angels but, you were left with peace inside.
Have you ever asked God if your prayers often go unheard,
And He gently reassures you that He always hears every word?

Often unanswered prayers are your ticket for greatness in store.
The things you thought you wanted - now you're blessed with so much more.
So you just might wanna thank God for requests He didn't fulfill.
Farther on down the road you'll understand it was God's will.

- Carol J.Hagan

What God Can Do

When it seems as though security is sinking low,
I call upon my God - because all things He knows.
When it seems as if being taken for granted,
I depend upon in whom my hopes are planted.
When a friend seems to be less than I hoped they would be.
I turn to the friend who is closer than a brother - never forsaking
me.

My security could never come just from a job.
My worth is of such value - that no one can rob.
Friendship of the Lord will never fade.
I am one of His creations - which He has truly remade.

No matter what man will do to me;
Use me for their own advantage under pretense - thinking I can't
see.
All the while I keep them in prayer - the ones whom spitefully use
me.

I never let on I can see past their veil.
Still, I keep praying - maybe someday they will be able to tell.
I pray that when they do - they themselves will ask,
"Why did she stick by me with how I treated her in the past?"

What God can do is a mysterious thing.
He uses our own faults, placing others to open our eyes - it seems.
Next time, to another, you are not being a real, true friend,
Realize the other could be a tool being used by the Only True
Friend.

- Beverly S. Harless

God's Blessings on Us

Your bills are paid monthly - you're not living on the streets.
You have clothes on your backs, and you have plenty to eat.
You have money in your pockets, even if it's not that much.
God's constantly sending blessings, to each and every one of us.

Your kid isn't an alcoholic, nor are they strung out on drugs.
You haven't been attacked, stabbed, shot or mugged.
You have instant lights, with the flip of a switch.
Yes, God blesses us daily, with every bit of this.

You have some type of shoes, to wear on your feet.
When winter is harsh, you have an abundant supply of heat.
You are gainfully employed, that's a blessing in disguise.
You're surrounded by loyal friends, that's always by your side.

When the summer time rolls in, and those temps are scorching hot,
You're blessed to have ac, that's more than others have got.
You always have plenty of water, to cook with and to clean.
Remember God is the reason, behind all of these things.

When you lose your faith in mankind, in God keep your trust,
Cause God's always pouring out, some kind of blessing on us.
You're blessed with God's mercy - and forgiveness when you sin.
There are so many others, in worse shape than you're in.

- Carol J.Hagan

Where Did They Go

Where did they go - the ones whom you served diligently in
ministry with for so long?
The ones who were closer than brothers - as you set beside them
and sang praise songs?
The ones you depended on to live up to what they claimed to be;
In your hardest times - they are nowhere to be seen.

As you endure what they pray they never hope they will -
Regardless of your circumstances, you are who you were - still.
You may have stumbled for a moment from the trial that you face.
But, God is still with you - He has put you in this place.

Alone and deserted - where did they all go?
When asking for help - their answer is, "N0".
Why can't they see, you need compassion and peace?
You question yourself, "Are they what they claimed to be?"

Feeling as if you are in a thick fog -
At least today - soon you will be standing so tall.
In the end, it is you whom has walked through the fire.
And it will be you whom will help another through their own
personal trials.

Look to the Master and the one in control.
You are in God's hands and He'll never let you go.

- Beverly S. Harless

Unpleasant Actions of People

Why are people so hard-hearted, and cruel to each other,
When the Bible plainly teaches us, to be good to one another.
Why do people think, they're too good to compromise,
They can be so uncaring, many times I've wondered why.

Why do people think, everything should be their way,
And to meet in the middle, would ruin their perfect day.
Why do people think, that they are always right,
And with their last breath, they choose to argue and fight.

Why do people think, everything is all about them,
That they're all that matters, they're often too quick to condemn.
Why do people get a thrill, when others they are bashing,
In reality they need to focus, on their own heartless actions.

Why can't people just be nicer, and strive to get along,
And just act their own age, since they're suppose to be grown.
Throwing a temper tantrum, and the words they throw are cold,
They can be so immature, reminding me of a two year old.

There's just too much compassion, that's out there to be found,
So don't go throwing stones, or putting others down.
I don't see how these trouble makers, even sleep at night,
As for me I sleep like a baby, cause I was raised to treat folks right.

- Carol J.Hagan

Around The Table

As we gather around for our Thanksgiving meal,
We will reflect on our family and love that is real.
Hard times endured and blessings beyond compare.
Each family's story is unique and each is rare.

In spite of our differences or conflicts we have shared,
Love abounds, binds - never changing - so rare.
Victories conquered from what the year has thrown,
Have made us wiser, life richer - we have truly grown.

Changes have been made since we last gathered around,
To give thanks to our Savior as our heads we bow down.
Tears will be shed for loved ones who no longer can share,
In the festivity of this holiday - it doesn't seem quite fair.

Knowing they are still there in our heart and our mind,
We focus on holidays past - never leaving them behind.
As we put aside harsh words spoken throughout the years,
We give thanks for what matters - eyes filling with tears.

Happy Thanksgiving to all, who reads,
Let forgiveness and thankfulness heal all - from these things be
freed.

- Beverly S. Harless

When I'm Old and Grey

When I am old and grey, and not so sure of where I am,
Will I be intolerable, or be as humble as a lamb?
Will I still be very capable, to live on my own,
Or will my final days, be spent in a nursing home?

Will my child visit often, and the others in my family,
Or will they be too busy, and not have time for me?
Will the days seem to me, to be forever long,
Will I just sit and wonder, where all of the years have gone?

Will I be pleased with how I spend my days, content, happy, and
care-free,
Or will I be like many others, wondering if I should buy meds or
eat?
Will I live for the third of each month, like so many seem to do,
Or will I have enough money, to live exactly like I want to?

Will I just end up lonely, or feel like I've been betrayed,
By all of the thousands I have helped, back in my younger days?
Will I have more time to help others, read the Bible more than I
did?
Yes I wonder when I'm old and grey, did I live like I should have
lived.

- Carol J. Hagan

The Unknown

Each day we face walking into the unknown.
To find a friend, make a difference in each and every home.
We depend on God to be right by our side,
For the occasions when a visit, doesn't seem to go just right.

His strength gets us through to finish our job.
He gives us strength even though we may want to sob.
Keeping us calm and holding our tongue -
Even when we want to quit and from that home run.

He reminds us we are a son or daughter of the King.
Nothing can touch us because, of what, to the situation He brings.
Showing God's grace through these times can change someone's heart.
In the end, it may be them God rebuilds from the start.

Regret and embarrassment is a tool He uses for conviction to start.
Starting them on the road - so His family they can be a part.

- Beverly S. Harless

God Always Looks Out For Me

If someone calls and tells you, that I'm broke down on 95,
Since the car on the side of the road, was identical to mine.
If you get another call, saying that I've been in a wreck,
Don't worry your little head off, don't panic and don't fret.

If someone says I've been diagnosed, with a life-threatening
disease,
Once again please don't worry, cause it surely wasn't me.
If you heard that someone, came and broke into my home,
Took all of my possessions, while I was asleep or gone.

That burglarized home, well I know it wasn't mine,
Everything is still intact, to me it looks just fine.
If you hear I'm unemployed, not a word of it will be true,
There's too many depending on me, there's so much I still need to
do.

I'm not saying that I don't face hardships, like others in this world,
But you can bet your bottom dollar, that I'm one protected girl.
When it seems as if there's to much, piled up on my plate,
God steps in and helps me, in Him I have so much faith.

So if you hear that any of this, is going on in my life,
Take it with a grain of salt, collect your thoughts and think twice.
God protects me daily, from all of the evil folks,
He travels with me in my car, yes everywhere that I go.

He keeps me pretty healthy, when all others are falling apart,
He guides each step that I take, He lives within my heart.
I know so many people, and their prayers I always receive,
Therefore I'm always okay, cause God constantly looks out for me.

- Carol J.Hagan

Your Testimony

What does your testimony mean to you?
Do others really see Christ in all you do?
Is your own family treated as well as your friends?
Or do you judge them harsher because they are your kin?

Have you estranged yourself over some silly little thing?
Or are you as forgiving as others, letting reconciliation ring?
Do you judge yourself as you do the ones that you judge?
Are you harboring resentment by clinging on to a grudge?

Can you understand that treating loved ones as strangers -
You are placing your testimony in unwanted danger?
Why can't you see it could turn others from Christ -
Making them feel as if it is something they do not want in their
life?

Is a stumbling block what you have placed in other's path,
Making it harder for them to grow and making sorrow last?
Do you realize it's not to them you will have to answer one day?
How will you explain your actions to Christ - what will you say?

Are you being what you claim in "all" that you do?
Christ looks at your "whole" heart - not to the good, to some that
you do.

- Beverly S. Harless

Through The Eyes of God

Through the eyes of God, the world is a different place,
What was once created so perfect, has become a total disgrace.
Through the eyes of God, this world has surely changed,
Removing His name from so many things, and we only have
ourselves to blame.

Through the eyes of God, people have stooped so low,
Forgetting all that they were taught, and forgetting all they know.
Through the eyes of God, the government fails us all,
They think that they're unstoppable, but in reality it's God's call.

Through the eyes of God, some doctors are heartless and cold,
Money is more important, not the lives of the young or the old.
Through the eyes of God, lawyers will one day pay,
How can a man be found innocent, when a five year old he raped.

Through the eyes of God, today's mothers are just unreal,
What kind of a mother leaves her child, some mothers even kill.
Through the eyes of God, dads aren't what they use to be,
What happened to till death do we part, and good ole fashion
honesty.

Through the eyes of God, most aren't what they need to be,
That list is for everyone, and that's including you and me.
Through the eyes of God, some churches are filled with pride,
And through the eyes of God, so many will be surprised.

- Carol J.Hagan

My Portion

The Lord is my portion, though all else fail.
I've been down to nothing - so many times I can't tell.
A door always opens, leading where He wants me to go.
His help is always present, as long as I don't tell Him no.

My strength and protection comes only from Him.
Both things He supplies when my world looks grim.
The valley stays only last so long.
Then to the mountain top He moves me to keep me strong.

Sickness has no power as long as He is on my side.
In the shadow of His protection, I can abide.
Trials and tribulations, just can't win.
All things are in His control, through it all I can grin.

Peace and comfort are in His mighty Word.
Depending on Him, I can soar like the birds.
A home He has prepared, so I'll wait 'til that day -
When with Him forever is where I will stay.

No matter what happens, right now in this day -
Faith is all that is needed allowing me not to stray.
Praise from morning until darkness turns back into light -
I know all the while, He is here by my side.

- Beverly S. Harless

God

The Alpha and Omega, the beginning and the end,
My all time trusted companion, my most reliable friend.
The One that watches over me, when I am sound asleep,
The One who dries my tears, every time He sees me weep.

He's the One who protects me, on these highways that I ride,
And no matter what cards I'm dealt, He's always by my side.
The Creator of the universe, the Creator of it all,
He tenderly picks me up, when I stumble or when I fall.

He is undoubtedly the way, and the truth and the life,
He's present at every birth, always there when someone dies.
He's the anchor that keeps me grounded, during life's stormy seas,
He hung there on Calvary, for the sins of you and me.

He's there when I feel helpless, always there when I feel alone,
He's the foundation of my strength, that makes me continue on.
He lives in my heart, I strive to be more like God.
If I keep it all together, I'll be where Angels only trod.

- Carol J.Hagan

By His Stripes

By His stripes I am healed -
He has renewed my will -
To carry on through this life -
Given me strength in my strife.

Peace and comfort unknown -
Carried me through in His strength alone -
So now others I must tell -
Without delay, without fail.

There is nothing He can't do -
If your heart believes in His truth -
Of His promises in His Word -
When with your heart you have heard.

Give your troubles to God -
In His strength no problem can trod -
Every second that is good -
Give Him praise as you should.

Give praise for the good days -
Ask for His help when you pray -
He is faithful and true -
And deeply wants the same from you.

- Beverly S. Harless

Things That's Unfixable

Some things are just unfixable, and that's really sad to say,
You take that broken heart, it often stays that way.
The words you speak in anger, sometimes they can't be fixed,
No matter how hard you try, that's just how it is.

A vase can't be fixed, and neither can broken glass,
Some things you did in your youth, although they're buried deep in
your past.
A roof can be repaired, but not fixed for very long,
When the hurricanes come calling, you'll need to put another one
on.

Alzheimer's can't be fixed, you wonder what's behind their smile,
Sometimes they seem content, other times they cry and cry.
Blindness can't be fixed, you spend your life without your sight,
Darkness can't be fixed, until the morning light.

Betrayal can be forgiven, but rarely is it totally fixed,
Somewhere in the back of your mind, you'll always remember this.
Death is also unfixable, we're all born to face that day,
Bad weather is unfixable, it often stays and stays.

A wasted day is unfixable, cause once it's gone it's gone,
Some types of strokes just can't be fixed, once the body is drawn.
Throwing stones is unfixable, since they cannot be retrieved,
Growing old is unfixable, although some choose not to believe.

Some relationships are unfixable, no matter what you do,
Wasting precious moments, you blaming him, him blaming you.
Yes some things are just unfixable, and that can be a shame,
Some things we can't control, many others we are to blame.

- Carol J.Hagan

This Christmas

This Christmas is different than any other before.
No tiny little feet will patter across the floor.
Only a young, lovely lady with many days ahead -
Will join us by the tree, after getting out of the bed.
Somewhere in the midst of presents and gifts,
A glimmer in her eyes - of the child she was - will lift.
Warm hugs and "thank you" she'll do just the same -
As in Christmas mornings past, after getting a doll or a game.
Maybe a surprise or two will catch her off guard,
Holding back tears - she may even find hard.
As I sit there and watch, I know I won't be able to hold back -
All the memories in my mind of every Christmas that has passed.
The first stuffed animal, she held so close -
Her favorite dress - she wore more often than most -
The earrings and necklace of her December birth -
Not believing she had gotten something of that much worth -
All the decorating and baking as she grew older, she complained about-
None the less eating all the goodies - "Leave some out for Santa", she would shout.
The look in her eyes as she smiled at the Christmas tree lights -
Popcorn, hot chocolate, watching White Christmas on Christmas Eve night.
I wonder if she ever guessed or even really knew -
My most favorite Christmas gift was watching her (year after year) as she grew!!!!

- Beverly S. Harless

When I'm All Grown Up

One day I won't worry you, tracking mud in on my feet,
And you won't have to carry me, from the car when I fall asleep.
You won't have to console me, when I have a nightmare,
And you won't have to help me, find my favorite teddy bear.

You won't have to see, that Kool-Aid smile on my lips,
Or discipline me sternly, when I throw my childish fits.
You won't have to rock me, when it's time to go to sleep,
Nor will in your bed, in the middle of the night will I sneak.

No more peeking in on me, when I'm lying in my bed,
No more bedtime stories, that to me you read and read.
You won't have to hide those Easter eggs, be the Fairy, or Santa
Claus,
You get to take a well deserved break, from having to do it all.

No more will you have to sew, or patch holes in my jeans,
No more set in grass stains, will you then have to clean.
You don't have to go school shopping, or purchase school supplies,
Or four pairs of shoes, and jeans and shirts of every kind.

You won't have to wash chocolate, off of my little face,
And not have to remind me, before I eat to say grace.
No more dreaded hours of homework, will you have to worry
about,
No more will you ground me, when I start to sulk or pout.

There're won't be any more sleepovers, with way to many friends,
No more ball games and parties, will you see me attend.
No more going to the park, just to feed the ducks,
But I'll never forget all you did for me, when I'm all grown up.

- Carol J. Hagan

My Mind Drifts Back

Now and then my mind drifts back.
I think of these times - just to keep me on track.

I relive in my mind the day my Father died.
Keeping his memory alive - oh, how hard I try.
Blinking his eyes to answer, "Yes" -
When I asked him if he wanted to experience God's best.
Watching the tears stream from his eyes,
After giving His life to Jesus - just hours before he died.

Going to grandmaw's each and every weekend,
Honestly, she was my very best friend.
She took me to church and taught me to pray.
Told me I would be doing God's work - one of these days.
Taught me that strength comes from above,
Made sure I knew all the verses that spoke of God's love.

Sending my child off for her first day of school,
I knew there, God would look after her, too.
Walking the aisle to the front as she grabbed and pulled,
For me to accompany her to the alter for salvation was so good.
Crying in silence as I watched her be baptized,
There were not enough tissues to keep my eyes dried.

Hearing my husband and watching him stand so tall -
The day he surrendered all and answered God's call.
Seeing the reaction of the neighborhood,
As he went door to door reaching all that he could.
Being amazed when he interrupted a basketball game,
When the players bowed their heads as they prayed in God's name.
As a plea sounded out after he walked away -
To come and tell another that Jesus is the way.

Nothing compares to when my drifts back.
When I start to lose my way - these things keep me on track.

- Beverly S. Harless

Old Folks

He gets up before the chickens, he goes to bed with them too,
All day long he's busy, doing things he needs to do.
She goes to bed with him, but gets up before he does,
To make him his breakfast, and the coffee that he loves.

She cleans up the kitchen, while he rambles on and on,
He swears a man's work is never done, not after you are grown.
She sweetly says a woman's work, is never totally done,
He takes her out on Saturday night, she's still his only one.

They go to church together, always sitting side by side,
After the service is over, they go on their Sunday ride.
Sometimes they visit the shut-ins, then stop at the Dairy Queen,
He takes her hand and whispers, "you're the sweetest I've ever
seen".

They are always together, no matter where it is,
The relationships today, can't even compare to this.
They vowed to grow old together, and that they have done.
I wish that I could see their love, in each and everyone.

- Carol J.Hagan

For What You See

I hear the giggles - see the cutting eyes.
As I walk in a room - it's no surprise.
The clothes I wear - just don't compare.
None the less, they are a blessing from those whom shared.
The newest styles - I can't buy.
Don't know if I'd even give them a try.
My hair is long and I keep it pulled back.
It would be nice if you didn't giggle and cut me some slack.
My car is not new - but that's no surprise.
I improve my home - at least I try.
Computers and gadgets - I admit I am behind.
Even though I know - I have more time.
Shows on TV - no time to watch,
Going places - I'd like to give it a shot.
You've never asked why - since I seem so shy.
I'll tell you now - or at least give it a try.

Mother's medicines - they just cost so much.
I stay home when not working - so her life I can touch.
Daughter's in college and she needed her books.
More important to me is the way "she" looks.
Money for groceries - has gone sky high.
Five to feed is hard - sometimes we barely get by.
I can't forget the children at Christmas this year.
Giving them presents - to my heart is dear.
Although I work - it takes all that I have.
To take care of my family - makes me so glad.
Don't forget about brother - he's almost blind.
It takes a lot of money - and a lot of time.
Going to the doctor, helping to buy his meds;
Affording a house - with room for an extra bed.

For what you see - is the real me.
Doing without to do for others - is the way it should be.
I couldn't stand myself - if "they" looked at me -
And saw something other - than the way that God says I should be.

- Beverly S. Harless

Things Money Can't Buy

There are so many things in this world, that money simply just
can't buy;
A mother's gentle touch, or that sparkle in someone's eyes,
A friendship that's lasted thirty years, or a marriage sixty plus,
Or a relationship that's filled with honesty, love and trust.

You just can't buy a healthy kid, or an aging parent's life.
You can't buy true happiness, or the air you need to survive.
There's no price tag on God's scenery, He paints like none other.
You can't buy the closeness, between a sister and a brother.

Neither can you guy a clean conscience, but you sure can get it for
free,
By doing good deeds in life, and being the person you need to be.
You can't buy compassion, you either have it or you don't.
It's great you can't buy someone's heart, some people's you
wouldn't want.

You can't buy a child's laughter, or that smile on their face.
The greatest things in life are free - like a hug, a kiss, an embrace.
The most precious, expensive and most important things in life,
Are the things that no amount of money could ever, ever buy.

- Carol J. Hagan

Looking Back

Looking back at all in my life -
It is riddled with bad decisions that brought so much strife.
I had all the answers whatever did arise.
Satisfying myself, was my only and biggest prize.

Thinking of myself as I ignored those around who were in need.
Not knowing that when they looked at me - all they saw was selfish greed.

Wanting and getting - was what this world said was good.
Plagued with this idealism - I had all that I could.
Yet, nothing brought satisfaction - I still yearned for more.
Never did I think that what I needed - could be found in the Lord.

Thinking I was in control of all that did surround -
Knowing I had just been deceived - when my knees finally hit the ground.

I fought so many battles - no one knew except for me.
I cried to Heaven with lifted hands - so I could be set free.
Crying like a baby - the weight I felt fell away.
God took me as His own with a promise there I could stay.

Yes, hard times have happened since I fell upon my knees,
But, now it is so different - God goes through it all with me.
Strength and protection from whatever this world throws,
Whatever is coming at me - before it happens God already knows.

Now, I lean on His direction - I am deceived no more.
Nothing I face on this earth - can stand against my Lord.
I am a child of God - I am precious in His sight.
I let Him fight all my battles - and it fills Him with delight.

So, I stand upon His Word - even if it's not popular to everyone.
I stand on the side of Jesus - My Father's Beloved Son.

- Beverly S. Harless

God's Residence

Everybody thinks God lives in Heaven, and I somewhat agree that's true.
But, He also dwells in people's hearts, ordinary folks like me and you.
He lives in a mother's touch, as she's holding her newborn.
His living quarters are in the smiles, of each and everyone.

God lives at all of the hospitals, and in a room that's filled with death.
He lives in the hearts of the poor, and in hearts filled with greater wealth.
He also lives in your vehicle, as you travel the roads each day.
He lives in your home, where you hit your knees to pray.

God lives at your work place, and the vacation spots where you've been.
He's also present every week, no matter what church you attend.
He resides at the funeral homes, where you show your last respects.
He truly lives in the heart of a mother, as her child is laid to rest.

God has several addresses, other than His home beyond the clouds.
He lives in the meek and humble, and in people's hearts - no doubt.
So, if you have room in your heart, don't hesitate to welcome Him in,
And one day God will let you reside, where the best of the best have been.

- Carol J. Hagan

Being Afraid

The Bible says, what have I to fear -
Many passages ring this message loud and clear.
Each day we face new and challenging things -
As fear creeps in, we forget what they mean.

We can fret and worry of how to handle our tasks -
Or we can return to God's Word for strength in what we lack.
We can choose to give in and let worry take over -
Losing a battle as Satan laughs over our shoulder.

We can chose to pick up God's Holy Word -
Letting the Holy Spirit fill our mind of what we have already
learned.
Impossible is only a reason not to try -
But, faith mounts us up on eagle's wings to fly.

Learning not to lean on our own understanding -
And forgetting our weaknesses depends on what we are standing.
For those who believe in our Savior above -
We know nothing is impossible for those whom He loves.

These battles wage war against us each and every new day.
Depend on God's wisdom and strength - He will light your way.

- Beverly S. Harless

One Girl = One Thousand Feelings

One girl can very easily have a thousand feelings in one day.
One moment she thinks that she's in love, in thirty minutes she says, "No way".
One day she swears that you're the "One", then, shouts it to the world.
By the time the news gets around, she no longer wants to be your girl.

She can also go to sleep at night, and imagine walking down the aisle,
Wake right up out of the blue, and suddenly lost her glowing smile.
One day she says, "I'll marry you", within an hour she's changed her mind.
In less than thirty seconds, she discovers that you're not her kind.

She can go from a young lady, back to the days of when she was two.
In no time at all leaving you, wondering what you really need to do.
She can care about you one minute, the next hour she won't take your call.
There's really no need to text her, she won't reply to you at all.

You're supposed to know what she's thinking, when she looks you in the eyes.
She expects you to comfort her, the million times that she might cry.
You'll need to be more understanding, and full of patience, too.
Remember of all the guys that are in the world, she only has eyes for you.

She can also play hard to get, and even appear to be sweet and shy.
Or, she can be the life of the party, with tears falling from her eyes.
But, if she honestly loves you, don't waste your time trying to figure her out.
Girls are full of one thousand feelings, but she truly loves you - there's no doubt.

- Carol J. Hagan

Daughter of Mine - Alison's Poem

The day I was told you were growing inside of me -
Was the first time I knew that miracles can be.
Fourteen years I was told you could never exist.
Now for eighteen years I have loved you with bliss.

From the first time you moved seeming to dance to the music -
Pressing your foot so strong against my stomach it all but hurt it -
I knew you would be full of life and of laughter.
You've proved my theory right each and every day after.

Head strong and stubborn - God gave you this plenty.
But it's one of your strengths as well as other strengths plenty.
Bunting heads - we have done our share -
But, no doubt ever entered that our love was rare.

Through "boo boos", and sickness and broken fingers -
Broken hearts, disappointments - our love still lingers.
From kindergarten and high school at times you struggled through -
But, these struggles that God gave you - gave you a strength that was new.

We sang all the children's songs as we waited for the bus -
When no one was around except for us.
Watching White Christmas each and every Christmas Eve -
Eating popcorn with hot chocolate - in happy endings we believed,

Scary movies followed by sleepless nights -
Laying beside you to comfort afterwards gave me such delight.
Every body of water seemed to call your name -
As you would jump right in as if it were a game.

At times your actions almost gave my heart an attack.
Yet, through it all my love for you never grew slack.
For all the blessings you have given me through the years -
I thank God for them all - including the tears.

Now a young woman so confident and strong -
It's only a matter of time - before long you'll be gone.
Never forget that I was your first love.
The older I get the more I need your hugs.

You will always be the daughter of mine.
As you start your life remember all of these times.
Where I am you can always call home;
You are in my heart where you belong.

- Beverly S. Harless

Wishing Heaven Had Visiting Hours

I've often seen where people wish, that Heaven had visiting hours.
Do you really know what you'd say, if you were given that power?
Would you tell your loved ones, that losing them just don't seem fair,
And let them know you long for the day, to prove how you really cared?

Would you ask for forgiveness, for with them not spending more time,
And not a day ever goes by, that they don't cross your mind?
Would you visit a few minutes, or with them spend all day and then,
Would you be in a hurry to leave, like the many times you once did?

Would you reminisce of days long ago, begin with your first memory,
Of you and them together, what a great day that would be.
During the rest of your visit, would you have and have a blast,
Hug and hold each other, wishing this moment would last?

Would you dread to hear the words, "visiting hours are now over";
Trying to hold yourself together, while calmly keeping your composure?
Would you wish you didn't have to leave, their new home called
Paradise?
And, when your time was up, would there be tears in your eyes?

Sadly we all have to die, graves are full of different ages.
Just be sure your names in the "Book", when God scans the pages.
You're not promised any tomorrows, so spend each day living right.
Then you'll never wish to visit Heaven, you can stay there all the time.

- Carol J. Hagan

Invisible

Each day, we do what we much do.
Though others are around - they don't have a clue.
They know our names and what our titles are.
But, in getting to know us - they haven't gotten that far.
The public "us" - we strive our best to do.
Yet, the ones who "know" us are only a few.

We care for parents and are raising our kids.
Some reach others for Christ and our "old selves" we have rid.
Our hearts are burdened for the ones who are lost.
Praying day after day - they are freed form sin's cost.
Others are looking for what this world leaves them thirsting for.
Not realizing Christ is knocking at "their" very heart's door.

All the while, the true calling for our lives are lived out and hardly
ever seen.
It's the quiet way we show - in whom we believe.
Gently guiding and persuading toward what we pray for them each
night.
We silently cheer as they slowly step toward a Godly life.
It's the invisible things that we do that are never seen,
That can lead others to Christ - so to Him they may cling.

- Beverly S. Harless

Twenty Years from Now

Twenty years from now, will I be in my mother's shoes,
Will I know who I am, or wonder who is who?
Will I display her disposition, and always wear a smile,
Will I be as humble, meek and mild, and remain half as kind?

I wonder if I'll know my daughter, and when she visits me,
Will it break her heart like it's breaking mine - I wonder how she
will be?
Will she then truly understand, all that I'm now going through,
If years down the road, she sees me in my mother's shoes?

Will I then still be able, to write a poem or a song,
Will I still know how to sing, when others sing along?
Will I still play the piano, or any other instrument,
Or, will I reminisce of times before, and wonder where my talent
went?

Will I remember people's faces, but just can't recall their name's,
I wonder who will be my voice, if my mother I became.
Will I have the same kind of, compassionate and caring staff,
What if one day I'm in my mother's shoes, I often wonder about
this and that.

- Carol J. Hagan

This Southern Girl

This southern girl is a God fearin' woman.
Don't treat anyone different 'cause we are all human.
I take a glass of sweet tea to my man when he's workin;.
I'd rather slow dance with him - don't like all that twerkin'.

I fix home cooked meals most every night.
I say what I think and forget it - no prolonged fights.
I admit when I'm wrong - to stay right in God's sight.
I thank God for His blessings and try to do what's right.

I happen to believe, a man is a man and should be treated as such.
And, that a man should treat a woman with respect - is not asking
too much.
My friends are also family and are welcomed in my home.
I help others during hard times - so they won't feel so alone.

I'm open about my faith even when others disagree.
I'm a southern girl - and you'll never change me!

- Beverly S. Harless

The Older I Get, the Less I Know

Eighteen years ago I knew everything you needed to know in life;
How to fix a baby dolls hair, and how to fly a kite.
I knew how to make a Barbie car, roll really, really fast.
I could make the best French toast, down here in the south.

I could make the warmest bottle, change a diaper the best,
Match clothes so perfectly, I could pass every test.
I gave the best baths, and I could cure any boo-boo,
With just a hug and a kiss, and of course a band-aid or two.

I knew all the answers, for her homework each night.
There wasn't anything, that I didn't do right.
I could handle any problem that she was up against.
Seems to me like now, I've just lost all my sense.

How I lost all my knowledge, I guess I'll never know.
What I once upon a time knew, she thinks I lost long ago.
I've driven a car at least forty years, all of a sudden I can't drive.
I'm tell you straight up, now I do nothing right.

Now I'm so much older, and it's so amazing to me,
All the things she once thought I knew, now I don't know a thing.
She now has all the answers, to everything in the world.
The older I get the less I know, and she's the smartest eighteen
year old girl.

- Carol J. Hagan

When In Need

When someone tries to help you, do you try to dictate their time?
Or willing to accept their deed - whatever time will be fine?
Do you treat them as a servant - although you don't pay them a dime?
Or complain because you're not the only one they help out, acting like they are committing a crime?

Are you as gracious and humble as the ones who cater to your needs?
Or do they feel a welcome relief as they close the door to leave?
Do you greet them with a smile as they enter your front door?
Or, do you act as if they are a bother - because they can't do any more?

Are your words uplifting - do you compliment their skills?
Or, is your attitude lacking - so that a giving spirit it kills?
Do you realize that "their" family is home waiting for what to you they give?
Did you know that doing for others isn't a job but how they live?

- Beverly S. Harless

Old Friends

Old friends know so much about you; the good, not so good and
the bad.
They keep life-long secrets, of all the crazy times you once had.
Some are closer than a sister, and stick closer than a twin.
Some you'll forever make memories with, time and time again.

Old friends come to your rescue, no matter the time of night,
To comfort and assure you, that everything's gonna be alright.
If you have a flat, twenty-five miles from home,
Old friends are the first to say, "I'll be there before too long".

When you decided to settle down, and it's your wedding day,
Old friends step right up, to help out in anyway.
The birth of your little girl, old friends are at your side,
Telling you, you can do this, wiping tears as you cry.

When your grandmother's dying, old friends know what to do,
You support each other, since they called her grandma, too.
No matter the obstacles, you're faced with in your life time,
Old friends are the best, I hope everyone has one like mine.

- Carol J. Hagan

It Just Might Be Me

I'm considered to not be living - though I am inside of you.
I don't know how I got here - and that's the honest truth.
I have heard some rumors - you don't want me here.
Even though I am unborn - I want to shed a tear.

There's one thing - I think is really unfair.
Someone else has cancer - they say it is alive and well.
The same for other diseases, as far as I can tell.
Even at the onset - they're so alive - they give their carrier a scare.

Why, can someone tell me - am I not alive, too?
I'd never do any horrible thing - on purpose to hurt you.
I progress just like those other things - until I am fully formed.
Why then am I not already living - as harmful cells in other forms?

I know it is your choice - but, my cells are not like the rest.
Nothing in me is harmful - you can try every laboratory test.
Although you did not choose me - or want me growing inside of you,
I could just be the only one in your future who may choose to take care
of you.

Someday other living cells - who aren't like me,
May also start to grow inside you - and there beside you I could be.
I could hold your hand and wipe your crying eyes.
I could be the one who listens - as you tell this world good-bye.

I could be the joy that you otherwise never could find.
If you'd only give me one thing I need most to grow....Time.
Sometimes, it is the dreadful things - or at least what you think to be,
That turns out to be a blessing - It just might be "Me".

- Beverly S. Harless

Special Moments

When my Mother says, "I love you", and she hasn't spoken in weeks,
When my dad takes the pulpit and he begins to preach.
When the Dr. says, "no chemo", the cancer is gone,
When my tiring day is over and I am headed home.

When I win a plaque that says, "Employee of the Month",
When I crawl out of bed each day, without a moan or grunt.
Those days when the office calls, and nobody there complains,
The days when my mind is at ease from life's pains.

When my child says, "I love you", and doesn't ask for a thing,
When I can catch a nap and the telephone never rings.
When a patient says, "I wish my daughter was as sweet as you,
And I bet that all your patients love you like I do".

When my six pound toy poodle, looks at me with trusting eyes,
The unconditional love he has puts me on the highest high.
When I walk in the door, he's one happy little boy,
Everyday moments like these, always fill my heart with joy.

When I open the mailbox, and I get a card and not just bills,
When for once I think I'm actually, doing what is in God's will.
When snow is covered on my street, and I get to stay home all day,
When I know I can face tomorrow, and not feel scared or afraid.

When my child calls and asks, "Can we go to the beach,
Like we did when I was younger, the days of just you and me?"
When the Carolina Tarheels win, especially playing Duke and State,
All of these special moments, puts a smile on this Southerner's face.

- Carol J. Hagan

A Spark in the Dark

Candles flicker as the say their good-byes.
Sobbing is heard as they lower heads to cry.
Pictures of the missing - they are desperate to find.
Until they know their loved one's fate - they will not rest their mind.
Pictures on the news casts played over and over again,
Messages on the voicemails that the missing did send.
Disbelief waves through each city, each home and each heart.
The attack on 9-11 was an awful shock.

Songs played on the radio as the months began to pass.
For our country, this memory, will only last and last.
The feeling in our hearts that we felt on that day -
As well as the weeks to follow, we should never let pass away.
Family became more important - the time we spend with them.
More people went to church and sang hymn after hymn.
Parents hugged their children every chance they could.
Husbands kissed their wives as often as they should.
Life had so much more meaning than in the recent past.
These are the feeling of 9-11 that should last and last.

My heart still goes out to the ones with personal loss,
On the day that the Twin Towers fell - they paid the ultimate cost.
Firefighters and policemen - many left their families behind,
As they gave their lives to save others from this awful crime.
Doctors and nurses saw sights they had never before seen,
As they treated all affected from the site's horrible scene.
The nation mourned together for what we did not understand -
A horrible, senseless tragedy that was brought to destroy our land.

The anniversary is upon us - as it is every year.
So, bow your head in silence and shed a silent tear.
Let family remain so precious - as they were on that day.
Be a spark in the darkness - and please don't delay.
No one knows how much time is left and when we will say our own good-bye,
For "all" the clock is ticking - let love be for what you are remembered as your
loved ones wipe a tear from their eyes.

- Beverly S. Harless

Pray For America

People have taken your Holy name, out of the public schools,
No longer are children expected, to follow the golden rules.
Some politicians had the Ten Commandments, removed from the court
house halls,
We use to be a United Nation, admired and we stood so tall.

Now, we're like other countries, with ungodly acts and numerous crimes,
People killing just to be killing, over something as little as your last
dime.
Children once respected their elders, but now they run the show.
I don't see things getting any better, since America has sunk so low.

If you discipline your kids these days, someone's eager to call 911,
I tell you, Lord, when I was growing up, that's not how things were
done.
We've fallen so very far away, from your precious Word,
People eat meal after meal, and no grace is ever heard.

Guess I'm old fashion but I don't understand, why the majority still can't
rule,
When atheists don't out number, all the millions that still believe in you.
Yet, they seem to get their way, and call it some type of "rights",
Good thing is, it keeps the Christians, on their knees day and night.

We don't have the right to ask for anything, or question you with whys,
But, when you look down from Heaven, there's gotta be tears in your
eyes.
From all the shame and humiliation, I'm sure most of us would agree,
Please forgive and help America, let it be grateful like it used to be.

If it wasn't for good folks praying, begging God to still help this Nation,
Everyone would be easily caught up, in all of the devil's temptations.
So, when you hit your knees tonight, and you begin to pray,
No matter what you talk to God about, ask Him to bless the USA.

- Carol J. Hagan

The Battle Has Been Fought

A wonderful family full of laugher and love -
God has given and blessed from up above.
A mother and father who were always there -
Dad ran out of time with us to share.
Heaven is where he now calls home -
One day I will be there, to see him is for what I long.

Mom is still here living the rest of her days -
I pray she, too, goes to heaven in honor and blaze.
Daughters are grown and have brought so much joy -
Many days left to see grandchildren playing with toys.

Husband spends each day by my side -
Sometimes, things get tough, but we always get by.
Heartaches and disappointment - there will be plenty, too -
But, by God's grace and sufficiency, He'll know how to sooth.

Grand-maw is missed each and every day -
But, she's singing with Dad giving God great praise.
Memories of her arise every new day -
With the sight of a red bird as it flies on its way.

Thoughts of how my Dad loved all his dogs -
Beau was their names - each one and all.
Our life has been blessed, I cannot deny -
But, one sweet day, we will again be side by side.

Heaven is where we know is our home -
As we wait patiently, it's for what our hearts do long.
Heaven holds so much more promise than this -
An eternity filled with only joy and bliss.

This temporary state we call our life -
Will be gone in an instant, away from this life's strife.
Tears will be dried and our bodies will mend -
Forever with our Lord and all of our friends.

When I am downhearted, you will still see me grin -
In spite of what happens, I know I will win.
The battle has been fought and has already been won -
By Jesus, my Savior - God's only Son.

- Beverly S. Harless

A Southerner's Delight

I thought last week's snow was something, let me tell you today is
a sight,
As far as the eye can see, it's a good ole Southerner's delight.
Snow at least six inches, and it's still coming down.
It's like a pile of white quilts, covering the ground.

There's no car tracks to ruin its beauty, everyone is sound asleep.
A cup of coffee in my hand, now that's the life for me.
Not one child goes to school and I don't have to work today -
Just lounge around watching the kids, playing on homemade
sleighs.

Everyone is excited and happy, as a child on Christmas morn.
All dressed up in their winter attire, trying hard to stay warm.
Before too long I'll fix breakfast, yes, I know that's quite a shock.
Afterwards I'll make snow cream, for everyone on my block.

For folks living in the south, it's that picture perfect day.
These memory making moments, I wish would never go away.
The fireplace is warm and glowing, every heart is at peace.
Of all the places in the world, home is where I'd rather be.

- Carol J. Hagan

Just a Sinner Saved By Grace

Please don't let others regard me for more than I am -
For I often make mistakes, as many as anyone can.
Don't let others give me praise for anything I should do -
Or for accomplishments I achieve or when I start things new.

Let my words always be seasoned with graciousness and love.
When I see someone hurting let me be compassionate to hug.
I pray that I offer when I see someone in need -
For that's what I would want - if the one in need were me.

When others reach out to lend me their helping hand -
Let me return the favor the best that I can.
Give me grace to be thankful for a shoulder that's lent.
May my eyes fill with tears for the helpers God has sent.

Never let me want anything I don't already have or need.
Let me find contentment and not be wrapped up in greed.
May the Lord break my heart for the ones who are lost.
Let me tell of God's love and How He paid sin's cost.

I am just a sinner saved by grace.
No more or no less than anyone else - any place.
Let me always remember I deserved salvation no more -
Than anyone else I should meet as I exit my front door.

Thank you, Lord, for the gift that you gave.
Please let me reflect you to those that I face.
I pray as I share and run my race -
That others see you through me - a sinner saved by grace.

- Beverly S. Harless

A Piece of Me

I give a piece of me to my dad, a piece of me to my mother,
A piece of me to my niece, and a piece of me to both brothers.
I give a piece of me to my job, a piece of me to my friends,
A piece of me to my nephew, a piece of me to patients time and
time again.

Another piece goes to my boss, another piece to my loving dog,
A piece of me goes to church, a piece also goes to God.
I give a piece of me to my neighbors, another piece goes to my
child,
A piece also goes to charity, another goes to a cause that's
worthwhile.

I give a piece of me to cleaning, a piece of me to my home,
Another piece goes to ironing, a piece of me goes to my lawn.
I give a piece of me to a stranger, a piece to whomever is in need,
A piece of me to my heart, so it will always do good deeds.

I give a piece of me to a nursing home, a piece of me to write,
Another piece of me I give, is to the homeless as I drive.
I give a piece of me to music, a piece of me to grieve,
By the time all the pieces are passed out, there's not much left of
me.

- Carol J. Hagan

Someday Soon

I am a simple person with a simple life.
Just like everyone - I have had my share of strife.
The mistakes I have made have been more than a few.
Some are still willing to tell them to you.

Never done anything special that amounted to much.
I've written some words and some people they have touched.
I will never be famous or rich by this world's measure.
But, I have built up in faith my Heavenly treasure.

I trust in God and I am not ashamed.
I have fallen to the bottom and called out His name.
I have been forgiven, redeemed and made new.
If you ask me my story - I will be glad to tell you.

I am a simple person with a simple life.
But, by God's grace, somehow I got things right.
You can try to discourage and tell me I'm wrong.
But, I've seen God's love and it is oh, so strong.

I know what I know and God has shown Himself to me.
By His death on the cross - He has set me free.
This world and it's problems are a temporary state.
And someday soon I'll meet Jesus - face to face.

- Beverly S. Harless

In My Daughter's Eyes

Many times I may stumble, and sometimes I may fall,
But, in my daughter's eyes, I stand so very tall.
There's not a problem, she don't think I can't fix,
No matter how many times, that I may falter and slip.

I have all of the answers, I give good advice,
Sometimes she takes it, sometimes she thinks twice.
She thinks I'm the smartest person, that she's ever seen,
Thinks I comfort her well, when she has a bad dream.

She thinks I'm her protector, knows I have her back,
Knows I won't let someone hurt her, or talk too much smack.
She thinks all her important crisis, I can somehow mend,
'Cause in my daughter's eyes, I'm the best there's ever been.

She thinks I can move mountains, when it comes to her,
And all of her bad days, I can magically cure.
Most importantly she knows, she's number one in my life,
And I ask God to forever keep me, standing tall in her eyes.

- Carol J. Hagan

Family Ties

Family should have very close ties -
Be close to each other when they are alive.
Searching shouldn't begin after our elders have died.
Sometimes, they can't be found, no matter how hard we try.

This is one thing wrong with the world today -
We don't seem to care from whom we have come from until our
ancestors have long gone away.
Whether uncles or aunts, cousins or further down the line -
We should know and take note of their lives while we still have the
time.

We should build our records while our family is close and hand
them down -
Not spend the latter years of our lives starting to look for the ones
who have been placed in the ground.
We have lost so much by not just taking good care -
Not cherishing our heritage and families while they were right
there.

Nonetheless, God has given us a blessing so sweet.
If we spread His Word, there's a greater chance we will soon get to
meet -
All the ones whom were unknown in our family line.
Time for family will last through out all of time.

So, get busy now while you still have years.
God's good news of salvation just might reach a relative's ear.
We may never know how much of our own family is reached -
Until we all get to heaven and see the rewards that came from what
we preached.

- Beverly S. Harless

Between A Woman and a Child

When your child is hurting, and you don't know what to say,
To make things somewhat better, or how to take her pain away.
When her eyes are filled, with way too many tears,
All you can really do, is let her know you'll forever be near.

When she don't want to talk, and holds the hurt inside,
If only she knew how I hurt too, every time I see her cry.
When someone disappoints her, or gets her hopes up way too high,
I reassure her that she's always got me, my love will never fade or
die.

When the love of her life, successfully tears her world apart,
And she's feeling like he finally, destroyed her once caring heart.
I know that she will love again, cause she's still so young in age,
If only I can get her through, this lonely heart breaking stage.

When friends and family upset her, and they don't follow through
with plans,
Her tender heart is just a beginner with life, way too young to
understand.
I try my very best to console her, cause that's my main job,
That's why I call her "daughter", that's why she calls me "mom".

Things were once so easy, when she was one or two,
A hug, a kiss, and a band-aid, instantly cured all of her wounds.
But, now she's eighteen, trapped between a woman and a child,
I pray God give me what it takes, to get her through this word
called life.

- Carol J. Hagan

Most Important Times

Been thinking about the most important times...
Time spent with family and friends come to mind.
Giving and receiving of deeds so kind,
Laughing with my brother as he is going blind.

Birthdays with daughters as they have grown,
Graduation celebration, triumphs we have known.
Walks on the beach as husband and wife...
All happy times spent throughout our life.

Simple times of laugher while just playing a game,
Meeting new people and learning their names,
Family reunions talking of times passed by...
Pictures of loved ones whom have passed, as we remember and sigh.

Days of summer spent drinking lemonade,
Memories stored for my older days...
A gentle breeze while sitting in the shade,
Watching my mother as her hair turns to grey.

Memories of my girls playing on the beach...
Hair in pigtails, chasing birds just out of their reach,
Fishing at midnight wrapped in blankets on the pier...
All of these memories, I cherish so dear.

Tales of pirates spin from sight of fishing boats...
As their lights rock on the water, giving the illusion of ghosts.
The most silly times and ridiculous things,
Stick in my mind and the memories ring.

Falling down upon bended knees...
Knowing from my sin, I have been set free.
Realizing my life is a gift from about...
Knowing God is with me and feeling His love.

For all good things come from God above...
All the things mentioned herein are born from within His love.
Yes, all of my most important times...
Is proof that my Savior's love doth shine.

- Beverly S. Harless

The Reasons I Love Mornings

It's that perfect time of the day, when all of the world is quiet,
Before you hear about, all the bad that happened during the night.
It's that moment it seems, as if the whole world is at peace,
Your body's fully rested, you've had a good night's sleep.

There's not that many cars out, it seems like the road's mostly mine.
Yes, I really love mornings, better than any other time.
Nobody's in a hurry, no troopers to worry about,
Nobody's driving like a turtle, that most perfect time no doubt.

I don't have to stop for buses, or that farmer creeping along,
I sit back and take it easy, as I travel from home to home.
Nobody's double wide is being moved, no construction crew in sight,
I can set the cruise on seventy, and get there in no time.

There's no garbage truck stopping, every fifty or a hundred feet,
No pedestrians walking or running, right out into the streets.
There's never little girls and boys, riding on their bikes,
Mornings are the best time, these are some of the reasons why.

It's before people that hate mornings, get on their naturally ill high,
Folks wonder why I love mornings, now you all know why.
It's seeing the sun rise, each and every day of the week,
I see the wonder of God, while others are fast asleep.

That's when I talk to Jesus, asking Him to help me along my way,
And if I do anything right, let it be to make another's day.
Lord keep me full of patience, keep me ever so humble,
And no matter how my day goes, Lord help me not to grumble.

- Carol J. Hagan

The Valley

It seems like forever when times are hard.
Yet, God is with you - standing guard.
He turns from your directions, worse things you can't see.
You can never imagine the worse things that could be.

God only allows you to suffer what He knows you can stand.
If not for His protection, your suffering would be much more
grand.
He goes before you, not allowing you to see -
Just how much He truly answers each of your pleas.

In the midst of the turmoil that is unpleasant to bare,
Know God is answering your prayers in ways you can't be aware.
Give thanks always to your Father above,
For the secret protection He gives you - because of His love.

When we don't see Him working is when He is working the most.
In the hard times of your life, of His love you must boast.
Be content in whatever circumstance comes your way.
He is waiting and wanting you to start today.

- Beverly S. Harless

Wait For the One

Wait for the one that will greet you, with a good morning kiss,
The one that tells you when you are apart, just how much you are
missed.
Wait for the one that holds your hand, no matter how big the
crowd,
The one that says, "I Love You", no matter who's around.
Wait for the one that really cares, when you have things to say,
The one that says, "NO Matter What", we will work it out some
way.
Wait for the one who believes in family, The Bible, God and you,
The one you trust with all your heart, in everything that you do.
Wait for the one whose eyes you look into, are only eyes for you,
The one you know will cherish your heart, and forever to you be
true.
Wait for the one who will never, bring tears to your eyes,
The one that will never crush your world, with a million of their
lies.
Wait for the one that has a caring, kind, and tender heart,
The one that makes your dreams come true, by wishing upon a
star.
Wait for he one that a simple hello, just takes your breath away,
The one that shows real love, in every word they say.
Wait for the one when you take those vows, to love and to be true,
The one you know is The One, and was sent from God to you.
Wait for the one who will stand by you, through richer or poor,
The one that spins your world around, the one that you adore.
Wait for the one that you can imagine, fifty years down the road,
The one you will one day whisper, "It doesn't seem like that long
ago".

- Carol J. Hagan

Pulling the Weeds From The Seeds

I look at all the Lord brings into my life,
Whatever trouble or triumph, it is always what's right.
Stays in the valley, then moving me to the top of the hill,
I find perfect contentment because it is all God's Will.

Each stay in the valley grown me more in my faith,
Even during these times, His grace is sufficient and great.
Molding me more to His image than before,
Leading me to move where He has opened a door.

When moving me to the top of the hill,
He has a purpose planned out that I must fulfill.
Teaching me to praise Him to others all around,
For turning unwanted circumstances upside down.

God is always faithful to supply what we need.
At times, it is something that we just can't see.
It can be unpleasant when God pulls our weeds from our seeds.
In the end, we're more perfected than we would otherwise be.

- Beverly S. Harless

What Heaven Is Really Like

Have you ever seriously wondered, what Heaven would be like,
Not the slightest tear, will ever fall from anyone's eyes.
You won't see a Mother will Alzheimer's, or a dad that had a stroke,
It will be like you won the lottery, you'll never, ever be broke.

You will never see cancer take the life of an innocent child,
The weather will always be fabulous, with temperatures just right.
You'll never see a dog, that was abused, neglected or starved,
All wounds will totally vanish, taking with them all of the hidden scars.

You'll never hear of rape, or anyone being gunned down,
This place is picture perfect, when you get there look around.
You'll never see a stabbing, or see someone strung out on drugs,
Never hear bad language, any swearing or someone cuss.

There won't be any diabetics there, no need for insulin or pills,
Hurting is not permitted there, therefore pain you will never feel.
To the ones on this earth, that was born without their sight,
The first face you'll see will be Jesus, what a Heavenly delight.

The cripple that relies on others, or his ride is a wheelchair,
Heaven just don't have a place, for any of that stuff there.
No hoyer lifts, no hospital beds, no walker and no canes,
In the blinking of an eye, so many things will forever change.

You'll have a heart that can't be broken, a love that will never fade,
There's no such word as loneliness, you'll be with loved ones every day.
You'll never hear about another war, taking your son to foreign land,
No hardships, struggles, or sorrows, you'll be a different woman a different man.

There's no volcanoes or earthquakes, no hurricanes destroying lives,
No homeless going hungry, nobody will ever be cold at night.
No child without their Mother, no Mother without her child.
Death is not allowed there, so nobody will ever die.

Imagine your life filled with, contentment, love and peace,
Your very own mansion, with pearly gates and golden streets.
If you'd like to live this life, there's no catch it's absolutely free,
And when you get to Heaven, by all means please look for me.

- Carol J. Hagan

Helpless

I have been to the place of nowhere to turn.
Weak and helplessness has made me learn.
Pain and suffering has its plan in God's Will.
For me it was to know, God was there - and to be still.

To reach the place where there was nothing I could do,
But, to ask for God's presence and for my spirit to be renewed.
To want nothing more than to be held in His arms,
To be shielded and protected - relieved from my harm.

Knowing that I had absolutely no control,
Desiring nothing more than to feel comfort in my soul.
I ran to the Father in faith of touching His hem,
Letting go of all things except my longing for Him.

In this moment I knew I was nothing alone,
All my power was useless…all my pride was gone.
As He wrapped His love around me and wiped my tears,
I knew all my knowledge was useless all these years.

I now know in my heart that without God I am helpless.
No power, no control…I am totally selfless.
All things, I had to place in God's capable hands,
For He controls all things…and I know now…that I can't.

- Beverly S. Harless

Through the Eyes Of An Alzheimer's Patient

When you wonder what I am thinking, as you gaze into my eyes,
I don't know what to tell you, the words rarely come out right.
When you ask if I remember, things of long ago,
Or things most recently, I'd love for you to know.
That your face seems familiar, your voice does, too,
But, I can't remember your name, or connect it to you.
When you ask why I'm crying, I really can't tell you why,
Or, if I've been eating, I just let out a sigh.

The nurses give me medicine, even though it's in apple sauce,
I often stare into a blank space, seems like I'm always at a loss.
For words that I once knew, it's like I'm two again,
But, once in a blue moon, I remember now and then.
Don't let your heart be saddened, when I don't know that you're
my kid,
Or, when I can't join in your conversation, like I once did.
When I'm not excited, about the gifts you bring to me,
The snacks, clothes, perfumes, the lotions, and the coffee.
I'd like to say thank you, but the words seem out of reach,
Just know that I'm grateful, with love that will never cease.
Give me the same patience, I had with you as a child,
Helping you learn to walk, I was there when you cried.
Sometimes I may stumble, and even hit the floor,
Just be there to catch me, like I did with you before.
You're the parent, I'm now the child, I know this don't seem fair,
Treat me like I treated you, full of love, kindness, and care.

- Carol J. Hagan

I Must Hold On

Within the valley there is such dismay.
Untruths surround - leaving me feeling betrayed.
No where can I turn to find someone with, to share.
For they join with the others - leaving all for me to bare.

Isolation is the target and it tries to take root.
Even in these times - I know the truth.
The reason for these things is plain in my sight.
Because I am grounded in God's Word and surrounded by His
light.

Darkness cannot cloud my views.
When the battles are waged, it's not ground breaking news.
For anytime I shall stand upon God's Holy Word,
Opposition will abound - opposers will surround like a herd.

I open my Bible and it confirms truth I've learned.
It makes me much more able for untruths to discern.
It gives me strength and I stand on God's Word through it all.
God holds me up, so I can still stand tall.

The Lord is my armor and on this Rock I shall stand.
As long as He's my fortress - I shall fear nothing from man.
All the battles of this world shall one day fade away.
But, the Rock that I stand on shall always stay!

- Beverly S. Harless

What an Awesome Childhood

My childhood was remarkable, although we were middle class,
But, we didn't know any difference, we grew up having a blast.
School always started, one week after Labor Day,
So, we could get the crops in, that just how we were raised.

Saturday morning cartoons, was an anticipated delight,
We only had three channels, but to us that was alright.
We all gathered around the tv, after breakfast at our house,
To watch Tweety Bid, the Flinstones and then watch Mighty
Mouse.

Foghorn Leghorn, Yogi Bear, and Casper the friendly ghost,
Looking back upon my childhood, I'm not sure which I enjoyed
the most.
Of course, there was Bugs Bunny, the Jetsons and the Roadrunner,
too,
Popeye the Sailor Man, then Shaggy and Scooby Doo.

Rocky and Bullwhinkle, Tom and Jerry, and Huckleberry Hound,
Spike saying, "That's my boy", the most protective dad around.
Porky Pig, Daffy Duck, Atom Ant, Pink Panther, too,
Alvin and the Chipmunks, oh the things those three could do.

We went to Church on Sunday, went to bed no later than eight,
We didn't talk back to anyone, we were nothing like kids are
today.
We didn't grown up with technology, just a tv, radio, paper and a
pen,
Still today's generation couldn't compare, to how my childhood
was back then.

- Carol J. Hagan

Tears

I rejoiced as I gazed into Jesus' eyes -
Full of peace and love, was not to my surprise.
Fear subsided and my joy grew strong.
Heaven was filled with praises to Him in song.

Streets of gold - there was radiant light.
My heart burst with excitement of Heaven's sight.
Not a single soul held a burden within,
Only smiles on the faces - every affliction He did mend.

What seemed to be just a short while from then -
Others stood before Jesus as the Great White Throne of Judgment
began.
My singing turned to silence as I saw them there -
As I looked among them, I saw family and friends.

Some I had told about Jesus and they chose to walk away.
Others I hadn't taken the time - then to my dismay,
When it came to the time - as each one stepped up,
To answer for that they had chosen - my shame was too much.

I saw each one I never told, turn their eyes to me -
As they were found guilty - for all eternity.
My joy turned to sorrow and I knew right then,
Not telling "ALL" was my biggest sin.

I fell to my knees at His feet in despair -
Realizing if I had done what I should have…many of them would
still be there.
Expecting to be punished, I raised my head in defeat.
Instead He cried along with me and extended grace so sweet.

- Beverly S. Harless

All in A Day Of Prayer

Tonya prays to stop smoking, Cheryl prays for her kid,
Carol prays to love her neighbor, like she once did.
Dianne prays for more patience, Cindy prays for her friends,
Melissa prays no more tickets, Joanne prays for her daughter again.

Belinda prays for her patients, Deborah prays for her girl,
Tony prays for more guidance, Beverly prays for the world.
Sherri prays for her husband, Emily prays for her son,
Jessica prays for all that depend on her, and that's everyone.

Tim prays he can help another, Shenita prays for her dad,
Heather prays for the relationship, that she once had.
George prays he stays off drugs, Helen prays she can keep her
cool,
Phyllis prays for her children, Taytay prays she finishes high
school.

Autumn prays she becomes a layer, Taylor prays she becomes a
nurse,
Amber prays she graduates college, Ashley prays she goes to work.
Elizabeth prays for her family, Dorenda prays to remain sweet,
Kristi prays to help every patient, that she will ever meet.

Denisa prays for all mankind, Debbie prays for her mother,
Tracey prays her life, will continue to touch others.
Donna prays that one day soon, she will win the lottery.
Daddy prays for my mother, grandkids, son and me.

- Carol J. Hagan

What Can I Say

I get asked most every day,
About where I have chosen to put my faith.
How can I know I've found the right place,
Putting trust in God, whom I've never seen His face.

All I know is I've found the right way,
Because of my Lord's saving grace.
I know it's hard to understand,
If you've never decided with Him to stand.

So, all I can do is, to tell His ways -
This is all I know to say;

When trouble mounts on every side,
I feel lost and only want to hide.
Grace appears when I need it most.
God send me a helper, His Holy Ghost.

He understands my deepest thoughts.
He leads me again to stand at the cross.
He takes the words I can't find to say,
Relays them to God, without delay.

When I'm perplexed and can't find rest,
When life seems as if it's just a mess,
Again, God's grace shows up on time.
It brings me comfort and peace of mind.

When I am weak and cannot stand,
He gently takes me by the hand.
He leads me to where I need to go.
Trusting in Him is all I need to know.

When sorrow comes and my heart aches so,
Before I say a word, He already knows.
He holds my heart with gentle care.
And, with me, that sorrow, He's there to share.

God helps me through each and everything.
Then He puts a new song in my heart to sing.
He'll always be my strength and shield.
To Him, yes, I will always yield.

He gives me joy that I can't describe.
Just knowing He's always by my side.
He makes me new - each and every day.
This is all I need to say!

- Beverly S. Harless

How A Southerner Talks

Up yonder, down yonder, up the road a spell,
Is shore is a scorcher, it's hot as wwweeeeelll.
Ain't seen you in a coons age, you're a sight for sore eyes,
Let's mend them there fences, and then go hog wild.

Let's get out them six strings, gotta pick them guitars,
Y'all join in singing, "How Great Thou Art".
It's time to get some shut eye, gotta be up at 3 a.m.
Gotta take out a barn, put anothern in.

Crop that tobacco, we got a ways to go,
Thank you Lord Jesus, we're in the short rows.
I'll carry you to the store, get some nabs and drinks,
Moon pies, RC colas, all them kinda things.

I'm fixin to cook supper, gonna make a heap of taters,
A mess of ham hocks and collards, and some fried green maters.
Gonna fry up a chicken, get me one from the yard,
Some homemade biscuits, with buttermilk and lard.

We go to bed with the chickens, get up with them, too,
Don't go getting your feathers ruffled, there's lots of work to do.
Get up younguns, there's a garden to chop,
I swonny, he's dummer than a box of rocks.

Gimme a washrag, gonna soap up that mouth,
Ain't no way to talk boy, down here in the south.
These dog-gone skeeters, bout to eat me up,
Wippersnappers, tying to catch lightin bugs.

Now don't go bite off, moren you can chew,
It's hotter than a wet settin hen, on a hot tin roof.
You've done ticked me off, barked up the wrong tree,
Don't go flying off the handle, if you still want them there teeth.

Oh, a bee stung your leg, sonny go get my snuff,
In no time at all, I'll have you all fixed up.
Cocolas and pepsi, is the drink down here,
At the filling station, you can get gas, smokes, and beer.

Today's our pig pickin, gonna cook us a hog,
Fire up that grill, get that charcoal and logs.
Get me a drop cord, cut off that light,
Don't ferget to say, your prayers tonight.

- Carol J. Hagan

When I Heard the Good News

Before I came to know my God,
I'd complain and moan about the earth where I trod.
Each time I heard something in the news,
Someone murdered or a child abused.
Natural disasters tearing lives apart,
I'd always been told God had a loving heart.

As time passed by, I wanted to try,
To find out why God let so many cry.
One day in the silence as I called out His name,
I remember it well, I've never been the same.
It was as if I could hear God inside of me saying these words.
I also remember that this time was the first time that I heard.

I am like you crying tears for these things.
I knock at your heart, but you ignore everything.
I've given the answer to all things in my Word.
You read them and think that it all sounds absurd.
Your own understanding is what you lean on first.
You have mocked me and ridiculed and some even curse.
You expect me to fix everything you see wrong.
If I did, would you even remember it long?
Bad doesn't happen because of my creation or my plan.
All things that are bad come from inside of "man".

If you'd change your path and come to me instead,
Let me change your heart and eat of my bread.
You wouldn't even notice that you lost anything,
Of any the things that you've loved - instead of me.
I will fill you with love and the desire not to do wrong.
Also, to tell others a love from me if what they should long.
All bad things from "man" would be no more.
If all would just listen and open the door.

You want things to change in this world, don't you see,
The only way to do it is to start with me.
You can't change the world if you don't change first.
Open your heart and quench your thirst.

- Beverly S. Harless

When You Meet Your Maker

When your days on earth are over, and you no longer walk this
earth,
When ashes returns to ashes, and dust returns to dust.
In the blinking of an eye, once your body is dead,
Where's your destination, is it Heaven or is it hell?

Did you ever help your neighbor, did you respect your mom and
dad,
Did you show compassion, every chance that you had?
Were you honest and caring, and kind to all you saw,
Did you give to the needy, were you a true friend to all?

Did you pray for your family, did you pray for your friends,
Did you ever pray for your enemies, or did you condemn?
When you were around others, did you let your little light shine,
Did you keep a clean conscience, night after night?

Or did you steal and lie, to everyone that you knew,
Did you use God's name in vain, or cheat on your wife, too?
Did you molest an innocent child, laugh while taking from the
poor,
Whatever you did for others, did you act like it was some chore?

Well then you have a problem and you better get this straight,
Do you want to experience hell, or walk through those pearly
gates?
Are you a Christian or a sinner, are you a giver or a taker,
Where will your soul spend eternity, when you meet your maker?

- Carol J. Hagan

What You Don't See

Many look at the cover - to decide what someone is like.
Most assumptions made from the cover - are hardly ever right.
Hardships and triumphs of another - you never can tell.
Looking at the surface - you only see their shell.

Some fought in wars to give freedom to you.
They never talk about it - they could have died for you.
Some nursed sick patients or loved ones - many days.
They never speak of their past struggles - it is just their way.
Some have deep wounds from the hurt they endured.
They'd tell you if you'd really listen - of this I am sure.
Some have lost children - way before their time.
Still, they hid what they went through - but, the hurt still chimes.

Some look at the outside - never seeing what is within.
Some disregard others - just for the color of their skin.
Some aren't on the same level - of fortune and fame.
Some look right past them - never knowing their names.
Some are not in our same social clicks.
Some treat them nasty - playing on them dirty tricks.

Many look at the cover to decide who someone is.
God looks in our heart and desires us to be everyone's friend.
We can not choose to whom - to show God's love.
He has already decided it should be everyone - from His throne
above.

- Beverly S. Harless

Winning the Lottery

If you ever won the lottery, what would you do,
Be ever so frugal, or go on a never ending cruise.
Take a trip to Australia, then maybe on to Greece,
Just point at a map, and go anywhere you please.

Go over to Israel, and walk on Holy Ground,
Be amazed at all the sights, there to be found.
Then visit Paris, be sure to see the Eiffel Tower,
Sip champagne, finish your day with whiskey sours.

Don't forget to visit Greece, have your honeymoon in Rome,
Take all the time in the world, getting back home.
Then on to Hawaii, see the islands in Mexico,
Spend money like crazy, everywhere you go.

Or, would you pay of your mortgage, mom and dad's , too,
Help the less fortunate, like your heart tells you to do.
Pass out lots of money, to strangers on the street,
Make sure the homeless, had a nice place to sleep.

Would you buy another car, maybe two or three,
Be a totally different person, from what you used to be.
Buy three or four houses, to accommodate each season,
Shop til you drop, without a good reason.

Would you visit the shut-ins, help change others lives,
Or, walk around proud, with your head held high.
Would you still have the same heart, you once had before,
You became a millionaire, wanting more, more and more.

Never have to worry about bills, or use a price scan,
Everything you want, at the palm of your hand.
Winning the lottery, would be a dream come true,
Decisions, decisions, tell me, what would you do?

- Carol J. Hagan

Daughters

From the day she was born, she captured my heart.
To guide and protect her, was my job from the start.
Teaching her what was right, from what was wrong -
So in the Lord, she could be strong.

I've guided and protected her from what goes against God's Word.
Throughout many years now, other doctrines she had heard.
I've taken those times to make God's Truth more clear.
To clear the confusion of other's beliefs put in her ears.

She learned how to pray and reference verse with verse.
Hidden God's Word in her heart, she rehearsed and rehearsed.
She's strong in the Lord, but she still makes mistakes.
But, what goes against scripture - she knows what is fake.

I've prayed all her life for her husband to be,
Godly, wise and strong and that he would see;
How we have raised the one he'll take for his bride,
That he'll put her first and not have selfish pride.

My job is about finished and I've done my best.
The man who takes over is responsible for the rest.
My daughter is special, she has known God's love.
He'll have no other option than to go beyond and above.

He must be an example for the rest of his life,
Continue to love her with the example given by Christ.
I gave her to God and she'll always be His.
For her husband - she is one of God's precious gifts.

If you are the one she chooses to wed -
You will have to answer for how you've led.
Continue to lead her in His ways -
And guide her so from His Word, she never strays.

You may love her now, but me, and He loved her first.
So, keep your promise to God of "for better or worse".

- Beverly S. Harless

Today's Generation

Today's generation has really gone, to the dogs and back again,
I appreciate how I was raised, kids were so much better back then.
They have no respect for the elders, not a drop of respect for themselves,
I'm here to tell you now, today's world is something else.

The 50's, 60's and 70's, produced some well behaved kids,
Even the 80's and early 90's, horrible things they rarely did.
Like shootings, stabbings, killings, or burning down a church,
My Mother would have surely beat, the living daylights out of us.

If we got bad grades at school , we and we alone were to blame,
Now parents run to the teachers, with false accusations and claims.
We best didn't talk back either, if we had any sense at all,
Kids these days think they're so big, their actions make them so small.

My Mother used to tell me, "There's no such thing as a bad kid,
It's parents not caring enough to raise them, the way I always did".
My Mother wouldn't have tolerated, one minutes of a kid's smart mouth,
She would've had a Come to Jesus Meeting, we wouldn't have like how it turned out.

- Carol J. Hagan

The Battle

It doesn't matter how hard I have tried,
Disappointment bombards from every side.
It tries to discourage from following God's Will,
So, I cannot proceed based on how I feel.

Negative words and acts sent to give dismay,
Things that go against the Words that God did say.
As these things try to penetrate against my fortress walls,
My God gives me strength to still stand tall.

As my enemies try to tear me down,
I drown them out as to not hear their sound.
I stay focused on my God above,
Since He has for me a never failing love.

When will they learn they do this to no avail?
As long as I stand on God's Word - they cannot prevail.
But, I will fight these battles with the armor He provided for free.
Knowing all the while, the war has been won because He fights for
me.

- Beverly S. Harless

The Fifties Mothers

She never went to college, her parents didn't have the funds,
But, she's admired, loved and trusted by at least everyone.
She's never owned a fancy house, she's never lived in a Condo,
Her home's filled with respect and humbleness, always a friendly hello.

She's never had hard earned credentials, that decorated her walls,
But, she was proud of who she was, the kind of mother that stands so tall.
She's never worn fancy clothes, they were mostly hand-me-downs,
But, she dressed in her best ironed clothes, whenever she went uptown.

She's never driven a Lamborghini, she rode in a '56 Chevrolet,
But, there's no doubt that Chevy lasted, longer than most cars do today.
She's never made a lot of money, some may even consider her poor,
But, she has priceless morals, nobody could ask for anything more.

She's never sought after fame and fortune, yet worth more than the finest
gold,
She's never put herself before others, so I've so often been told.
She never tried to outshine for praise, but oh what a shining star,
My prayer so often is to be, half the mother that you still are.

She's never had a chauffeur, a cook, a babysitter or a maid,
She's just an old fashioned mother, wish there were more like her today.
She's never worn expensive jewelry, but she's an American jewel,
I wish the modern day mothers, did mothering like mothers used to do.

- Carol J. Hagan

Importance of Work

Our work or job determines what we have in this life.
Rewards of our income determines what we will buy.
How big our house is, or the luxury of our cars,
The clothes we purchase, if we travel near or far.
Insurance to take care of us when we are not feeling well,
Gives us security in our mind that is hard to fail.
Our title or position defines whom we are to all.
Climbing the ladder of success leaves us standing so tall.
Ambition and drive to do the best that we can,
So, all the important things in life can be afforded - is so important to man.
We go the distance working weekends and nights,
Spending hours doing paperwork after the sun stops giving light.
Calling clients or patients - planning for the next day,
In order to make quotas that brings our much needed praise.
So much time and importance is put on our work,
We give no second thought to how much time that it took.
It is merely something that just has to be done.
It's a race of importance from were earthly treasures come from.

Yet, God has given all whom He calls His Son,
A more important race that we have been instructed to run.
Telling all that we see of His undying love,
Is the most important race that we ever will run.
Spreading the gospel of Christ is what He has given us charge,
In doing so, our Heavenly treasures will be large.
Will we be standing tall before the Judgment Seat,
Or, have nothing to offer as the Lord we greet?
Will we have to explain or feel such sorrow inside,
That our earthly race was where our time did abide?
Will we watch as our loved ones and even our friends,
Are sent away into torment because where our time we did spend?
As they are taken from the gates of where we will have perfect peace,
Will they be shouting, "YOU could have told me - at least!"
Will our heads hang in sorrow as never before?
Will we be ashamed to look upon our Lord?
Or rather, will we find comfort knowing we've spent more time in the race -
That impacted souls for an eternity instead of this old earthly place?

- Beverly S. Harless

Alzheimer's through the Eyes of My Dad

He never misses an anniversary, never misses a holiday,
No matter the occasion, he always steps up to the plate.
He never misses mama's dr. appointments, he's always by her side,
No matter when it is, no matter where, no matter the time.

He visits her faithfully, never misses a single day,
Nothing's gonna stop him, nobody's gonna get in his way.
He makes sure she's taken care of and that she's eating well,
If this 80 year old man ever tires, he would be the last one to ever tell.

He greets her with, "Hello darling, how are you doing today?",
Many days she grins and smiles, other times she's an emotionless face.
He sits and holds her hand, while she drifts off to sleep.,
What an amazing love they share, true love, so real - so deep.

He gently kisses her on the cheek, and reluctantly leaves her side,
She's always in his heart, forever weighing on his mind.
Often she don't know he's there, but that don't matter to him,
She still owns his heart, no matter what shape she's now in.

He opens his humble dwelling, and falls down on his knees,
Asks God for more understanding and to bless him with more strength.
He's surrounded by precious memories, of better days that he's once known,
He slept with her for sixty years, but now he sleeps alone.

He will be up way before day light, and start his same daily routine,
As he hurries to see my Mother, making sure she don't need a thing.
He takes care of so many people, always wearing that caring smile,
But, I also know the pain he carries, I see it in his eyes.

- Carol J. Hagan

Somewhere

Somewhere a child cries for a parent lost.
Maybe fighting for freedom - paid the ultimate cost.
A mother had cancer and fought as long as she could.
First, raised her children right - teaching evil from good.
A drunken driver crossed over double lines,
Leaves a child alone to face their life and hard times.

Somewhere a child cries for a parent lost.
Sometimes, it's the parent - whom their child they tossed.
Into the care of another who dearly wants them there,
Giving that child love unknown and showing they care.
They fill the void and give them a home,
Making sure that the child never feels alone.

Somewhere a child cries for a parent lost.
Yet, they all have a Father who died on a cross.
Some never hear and can't understand,
Because no Christian has taken the time to hold out their hand.
Afraid to tell the Gospel even in their own land,
Many it is they, who doesn't truly understand.

It's not about us and the parts we choose to believe,
When we open the Bible - we should believe all that we read.
It's about bringing others to our Father above.
It's about sharing His Word and spreading His love.
It's about bringing revival to a county in need,
It's about rebuilding it to what it used to believe.

It's about having something rock solid to stand upon.
Not what is gone tomorrow when something new comes along.
Knowing that it is the same today -
That it will last and last and will always stay.
Never compromising in even one thing -
Not filled with confusion, letting only Truth ring.

Somewhere a child cries for a parent lost.
They need us to teach them about that old rugged cross.
So, they can develop a heart for reaching others like them,
Making revival possible - not just a passing whim.
Let go of your fear and being politically correct.
Reaching just one - can cause an awesome effect.

Somewhere a child cries for a parent lost.
Won't you tell them of the One who paid salvation's cost?

- Beverly S. Harless

I Had the Meanest Mother

While other kids stayed up all night, I was in bed by seven,
While others rode the roads, my curfew was SHARP eleven.
While others ate chips and candy, I had to clean my plate,
I ate what was put before me, no exceptions were made.
While other kids wore short-shorts, you guessed it, no not me,
They even went to the movies alone, watched what they wanted to see.
I had to watch, "Gone With the Wind", "Ten Commandments", or a
cartoon.
And, if I misbehaved, I got much more than sent to my room.
We spring cleaned every Friday, so we could go out on Saturday night.
We didn't skimp on the cleaning either, it had to be done right.
While others enjoyed their summers, we barned tobacco and mowed the
grass,
Picked cucumbers, canned veggies, she made us do this horrible task.

She made us tell the whole truth, nothing else would work,
We knew better than to roll our eyes, or make the faintest smirk.
Whatever house she took us to, we'd sit there on the couch,
You never knew that we were there, we were quiet as a mouse.
We didn't dare go in their fridge, we didn't ask for anything,
We didn't think about jumping on the beds, didn't pitch a fit or scream.
She insisted on knowing our every move, and every friend we had,
And if we failed to tell her, it would be BAD, BAD, and more BAD.
If someone came to see us, they had better not toot a horn,
They had to be respectful, and knock on her front door.
I thought I had the meanest mom, but she must have done something
right.
We've never been drunks, or druggies, gone to jail, or been in a fight.
All because she was so mean, we didn't turn out like the others,
Who can we blame for this, you guessed it, my mean mother.
So, since she was so mean, and we turned out just fine,
I plan to be just like her, just ask this child of mine.

- Carol J. Hagan

My Way Back Home

It's been many years since I left my home.
I wanted adventure as I left to roam.
Wanting to grow and find my way,
Home is where I could not stay.
I shed some tears, but wiped them dry,
Hugged my parents as they cried.

Now, I'm trying to find my way back home.
This old world has left me all alone.
To have the comforts I once had,
Not wake to every day so sad.
Lord, please help me find my way back home.

With a broken heart and relationship,
I need something real to grip.
Things aren't as they once seemed to be,
Disappointments led to misery.
Once I had it all, or it seemed to be.
Feels like something died inside of me.

Now, I'm trying to find my way back home.
This old world has left me all alone.
To have the comforts I once had,
Not wake to every day so sad.
Lord, please help me find my way back home.

Mom and Dad are long gone now.
Tell me what to do, and that I shall.
Guide me and I'll follow you.
I'll do anything you want me to.
I don't want to continue on this path.
I need your salvation and a life that lasts.

Now, I'm trying to find my way back home.
This old world has left me all alone.
To have the comforts I once had,
Not wake to every day so sad.
Lord, please help me find my way back home.

Don't let me be the man I was.
Make me a man who demonstrates your love.
Let me be a light in the darkest place,
Lead others to your amazing grace.
Witness to the ones in need -
God, this is my sincerest plea.

Now, I finally found my way back home.
From your presence I will never roam.
Through your grace, I've found comfort I've never known,
And my heart is filled with joyful song.
Lord, I praise you - for leading me back home.

- Beverly S. Harless

A Day in the Life of a Trucker

Others may drive a few miles a day, and tell of things they've seen,
But, we've been places my friends, that's not in your wildest dreams.
Our day consists of 14 hours, driving up and down the interstates,
We rarely stop to eat or rest, these things just have to wait.

Fighting traffic on a daily basis, going through countless scales,
Making sure we're all up to par, so we don't go to Trucker's Jail.
Loading and unloading trucks, can really get to your back,
But, once in a while, if you're lucky, a fork lift driver will do that.

You often miss the birth, of your precious newborn child,
Your wife tells you on the phone, "She has your nose and eyes".
You miss her very first day of school, the first time she talked.
When she learned how to crawl, then when she learned to walk.

Holidays can be so lonely, someone's always waiting on a load,
We can't stay home with family, our life becomes the road.
You work in all conditions – snow, sickness and even when you hurt,
Gotta keep those wheels turning, that's the only way to make a buck.

Everything you have used in life - eaten, drank or have touched,
Has at one point been delivered, by the driver of some truck.
So, before you go to sleep at night, close your eyes and pray,
For God to keep all truckers safe, on these busy highways.

- Carol J. Hagan

My Heart

Just as anyone else does, I have some dreams.
In this aspect we are all the same - or at least it seems.
Family to be well - no illness in sight,
Children who are respectful - not full of hatred, fills our heart with delight.
Spouses who would give their life for whatever would bring harm,
To protect us, as God does - keeping watch for what alarms.
Closeness with loved ones - never losing touch,
It seems in this world though, this doesn't mean much.

God as our Father and being first in everyone's life,
This, too, it seems - is long gone from our sight.
Government making decisions based on God's Word as it should.
But, nowadays, this concept is just flat misunderstood.
Churches that are bold reaching everyone they can.
Not just sitting in pew a few hours - afraid to lift thankful hands.

Witnessing for what wonders God has done in our lives.
Not being afraid of being outspoken - remembering Chris died for this right.
Helping our neighbors when they are in need,
Instead, of being afraid they ask for help out of greed.
Spreading God's love to everyone - not just to some,
Not basing what we are willing to do because of where they come from.

Not playing God - by self decision of who gets to hear,
The Good News of the Gospel to someone who is different or be it our friend.
No one discouraging any one whom God has called,
To do His work - because "we" can't see it - that they would be called.
Just as anyone else does, I have some dreams.
Are yours the same as mine - or about "material things?

- Beverly S. Harless

Santa, Through the Eyes of a Child

Every child loves St. Nicholas, even when they seem afraid.
They know he's the one with the goodies, they all get on Christmas Day.
Their innocent eyes see him, as Mr. Perfect dressed in red and white.
The one that pays them a visit, once a year on Christmas Eve night.

They see him as the one, who grants their wishes and their dreams.
Yes, old Santa walks on water, they think he can do anything.
To them he's always kind and polite, asking what they want him to
bring,
He doesn't need to write it down, cause Santa remembers everything.

His reindeer is another story, they think they fly the very best,
In their eyes they're even faster, than any kind of plane or jet.
They know the reindeer by name, their favorite of course is Rudolph,
'Cause he's the one who leads the sleigh, when Santa Claus takes off.

The elves simply amaze them, cause they're feisty and full of life,
They look at them as playmates, since they are all the same size.
The shiny lights, the Christmas Carolers, snow falling, even mistletoe,
They look so different through the eyes of a child, even Santa's Ho Ho
Ho.

Just the mention of Santa's name, can stop a kid in their tracks.
'Cause they know they have to be good, to get what's in his sack.
There's nothing that's comparable, to their smiling face, no not to me,
When they wake up on Christmas morn, there's nowhere else I'd rather
be.

- Carol J. Hagan

Many Nights

Lord, I am in such anguish as I've never been before.
I can't sleep at night - every few moments my feet hit the floor.
I have one request - to not let my suffering be in vain.
When I think of others in anguish - there are so many names.

Each night that I am restless and the pain will not let go,
Let each night give another a night of peaceful sleep - is my hope.
If I must continue to suffer - let it be done to lessen theirs.
Let each one have a good night sleep - without pain and without care.

Let it be for the lady who has cancer and is afraid to close her eyes,
In fear that she may not wake - so she stays awake and cries.
For the husband who has lost his job and knows not what to do,
Doing every odd job he can find, just to make enough money for food.
Don't forget the parents worried about their child,
Facing what they never dreamed they would - it's such an awful trial.
Oh, I just remembered the ones who work diligently in Your Name,
Fill them with assurance so their faith will never wane.
There are many others that need a little break.
Let my suffering be done -for all others who suffer sakes.

Lord, I am in such anguish as I've never been before.
Please each night when every few moments, when my feet hit the floor,
Give another who also suffers your wonderful amazing grace.
I am sure that they will praise you - and some will seek your face.

- Beverly S. Harless

Housewives

You've heard that old saying, "A housewives work is never done",
Husbands often think their job, is 24-7 of nothing but fun.
They think wives watch Netflix, and can be found all day online.
They just sit around relaxing, and have a grand ole time.

They also think their wife, gets to lounge around all day,
After the kids are off to school, they think wives have it made.
Husbands are the first to tell you, "My wife doesn't work",
If they realized what wives really do, they wouldn't be such a jerk.

I wonder if they wonder, who cooked the food that they just ate,
Or, who just washed all the silverware, glasses, pots and plates.
I also wonder if they think, their clothes are magically cleaned,
And who makes sure they're always on time, that someone would
be me.

Yes, it's true you go to work, and I'm a stay at home wife,
But, I do more work in three hours, than you do from nine to five.
Let's not forget when you get home, you play games and watch tv,
I'm constantly doing something, till it's way past time to go to
sleep.

Now, when the kids are sick, it's me that sits up all night,
You on the other hand, slept thinking everything's alright.
It's now time for you to get up, and I haven't even been to bed,
Think I'll just sit here and do nothing, at least that's what you said.

- Carol J. Hagan

At This Time

At this moment in time my memory is clear.
I understand and acknowledge every word that I hear.
I can pick up the phone and call loved ones so dear.
We can laugh about silly things and at the bad, shed a tear.

I don't know what, for me, tomorrow will hold.
For my memory slips away at times, so I am told.
When it will happen, I never can know.
So, for now I will cherish this moment as gold.

They tell me that my future looks different for me.
I may not know your name, when your face I see.
It will be hard for you, for I won't remember most things.
So, keep these words in your heart and let them sing:

Everything that we once shared is a part of me.
It's the joy that shines through in spite of this disease.
It's the smile that spreads upon my face.
And, the giggle that slips when I am in a daze.

It's the things that we shared when I was full of life -
That God gave to help me through my strife.
So, think again on the memories, that we shared, that you now
hold,
For, it's my memories that are alive in the memories of "your"
soul.

- Beverly S. Harless

People That Don't Work

Some wouldn't work counting money, if half of what they counted
they got to keep,
They have all the necessities in life, yes everything that they need.
They have designer jeans and shelter, they also have lights,
They eat a lot better than I do, and I work day and night.

They own flat screen tv's, the smallest one's a sixty inch,
Those iPhones and iPads, to me it don't make much sense.
Laptops, desktops, and kindles, all of the latest technology.
Where do they get their money, they must own a money tree.

They wear Ray-Bans, Oakleys, and Costas, while I wear the
Walmart brand,
Something isn't right with this picture, I just don't understand.
They have a closet full of shoes, a different pair for each day,
The best of the best cell phones, at a price I can't afford to pay.

They eat out and go to the movies, at least once or twice a week,
If I go and buy their popcorn, then I can't buy their drink.
They have a car in the driveway, sometimes they have two,
I'm contemplating on quitting my job, I think that's a plan don't
you.

Before anyone gets bent out of shape, and thinks I'm a jerk,
I'm not talking about the disabled, just people that choose not to
work.
The ones that think the world, somehow owes them a living,
Where was I when they passed out, all this taking and no giving.

- Carol J. Hagan

How Others Can Tell

Start your day not thinking about yourself.
Do something for others that they see as heartfelt.
Bring a laugh or a giggle to all that you meet -
Regardless of whom it may be that you greet.

Show something different in the way that you live.
Let love radiate from you and let that love be what you give.
Compassion and concern may make someone's day.
Bring a smile to someone's face with what "your" lips say.

Instead of letting others control what your mood will be,
Lead them by example so they, too, will be filled with glee.
Sometimes, what you reflect - even if you are unaware,
Is exactly what others need to deal better with their own cares.

Without love and joy that emits truly from the heart,
We are bankrupt and helpless from the very start.
Find the spark that makes your love for others grow.
Let it grow until from others, it's what from you, they know.

Jesus said this is how others can tell,
We are His disciples - whether we be male or female.
Let your light shine and drive the day's darkness away.
If you do you many find that others may start making "your" day.

- Beverly S. Harless

The Hardest Words to Hear

The results came back positive, you'll need to take chemo,
It's confirmed cancer, off to radiation you must go.
Your mother's in excellent health, other than her mind,
Alzheimer's get the best of the best, way to many times.
Your brother had a stroke, he's only fifty-five,
If we don't control his sugar, in five years he's gonna die.
Your niece has to have heart surgery, even though she's thirty-three,
She could die on the table, we'll have to wait and see.
Your child was born premature, only five months old,
I did my best to save him and the tears start to roll.
Your daughter just had a wreck, on interstate 95,
We're doing everything we can, just to help her survive.
You'll need to make this decision, should I pull the plug,
Or, let her lie here helpless, I know you want what's best for her.

I want to leave home, although I'm still in school,
I no longer choose, to live under your rules.
I'm having a baby, I know I'm just sixteen,
I'll move in with my boyfriend, he'll take care of me.
I'm getting married, I know he's the One,
I cheated on you, my God, what have I done.
Yes, I'm pregnant, but you're not the baby's dad,
I fell for another, please don't take it so bad.
I think we need to break up, I just need a little space,
We can't get back together, I found another to take your place.
After twenty years of marriage, I want a divorce,
I'll take the house and the car, I'll see you in court.
I no longer love you, please go on with your life,
It just wasn't in the cards, for me to keep being your wife.

Life can be hard, lessons have to be learned,
Handle all situations, with the utmost concern.
Be slow to anger, always think things through,
If it be a long time investment, or just a dollar or two.
Before you rush to judge others, make sure your backyard's clean,
Putting God first in your life, will conquer anything.
Sometime in your life, you're prone to hear one of the above,
What outweighs all of the obstacles, is prayer and old fashioned love.

- Carol J. Hagan

A Daughter of the King

I am a gift from God above,
To all the male figures to whom I give my love.
Whether you be father, boyfriend or my husband in this life,
Still I am not perfect and at times may give you strife.

Be patient and loving as we share ups and downs.
There will be many times that our smiles will be frowns.
Yet, through it all, my love for you will never change.
To love you unconditionally, for me is gain.

We will both makes mistakes, making us unworthy of the other's love.
I promise to still love you with the ensample of love sent from above.
God still loves knowing we will always make mistakes.
This is how He has shown us to love our earthly mate.

I will hold you accountable to keep you right with God.
If I do not do this, I would not be doing my job.
I am not a help mate of just things of this earth.
I expect you to love me as Christ loves His church.

Respect and support I give you the rest of our days.
I promise you this, "Signed, a daughter of the King."

- Beverly S. Harless

Nursing Homes

There's good, there's bad, then there's all in between,
In a week's time, you'd be surprised at, all the things you see.
Mrs. Hinton is just sitting there, slumped over in her wheelchair,
Does the staff even notice, or do they even care.
Then there's Mrs. Johnson, down in room 203,
Her kids never visit, how lonely she must be.
Miss Pat was a music teacher, way back in ninety-eight,
She would smoke those ivories, oh, how she once played.

Mr. Smith sits outside, and smokes cigarettes all day,
He says, "Something's gotta kill me, so I can get out of this place".
Mrs. Wahl's son was killed in Vietnam, he was her only kid,
She showed me all of his medals, and told stories of all he did.
Then there's good ole Mr. Jones, flirts with every lady he sees,
His goal in life is to remarry, although he's ninety-three.
Let's not forget Mrs. Ester, now she's a piece of work,
Nobody every visits, she tries hard to hide the hurt.

There's Aunt Bernice close to the door, in room 105,
Everyone there loves her, she has the sweetest smile.
Down that long hall is Mrs.Joyner, she stays in bed 24-7,
Constantly praying that God, will soon take her to Heaven.
Mrs. Rook takes a nap early, for bingo she needs to be up,
To win her prized possession, a plastic coffee cup.
Then you have Mrs. Snow, she's the life of this place,
She thinks it's her duty, to put a smile on the patients face.

Let's not forget Mrs. Bass, she has a heart so kind,
Her health is failing her, still she has the sharpest mind.
Then there's Mr. Buddy, he watches westerns all day,
He never asks for anything, has very little to say.
Mrs. Shearin is the sweetest thing, that I have ever seen,
All she does is praise God, thanking Him for everything.
Then you have Mr. Burgess, his heart is made of gold,
He was once homeless, so he's thankful, I've been told.

There's a group of musicians, that go now and then,
To play country and gospel, and the patients join in.
There's Barbara, Linda and Diane, the very best C.N.A.'s
All taken into consideration, I really like this place.
The Med Techs are like family, Deborah and Ray,
Their cheerful attitudes, makes each patient's day.
I could search a hundred mile radius, and find no other,
Place that would treat my mama, like their own mother.

- Carol J. Hagan

The Plan

We cannot see the reasons why,
When we are told we have cancer and soon will die;
Or when so young and should be in our prime,
Why we are bed bound - there spending our time.

We may never know why or understand,
But, rest in the assurance it is part of God's perfect plan.
Faith in His purpose for all we endure,
Starts with praying for comfort and peace - in that I am sure.

The mustard seed is one of the tiniest seeds.
In the end, it is the strongest of all God's trees.
Faith of this size seems so small - I know.
But, just like the seed - it needs planting to grow.

It's funny what God can do with a small measure of faith.
His Word tells how with even this, His miracles can be great.
Whatever His Will - even if He chooses not to cure,
The faith that you show can change another life - for sure.

A grandchild, son or daughter, husband or aunt,
Could find salvation from the faith you did plant.
Remember the greatest of things, is giving your life for another.
The plan could simply be during these times - using your faith to
lead to God - others.

- Beverly S. Harless

My Beloved Dog

My mind goes back to the day, I bought you in ninety-three,
You were the tiniest thing, that I had ever seen.
You were cute as a button, you were also black as tar,
You could hardly wait that day, to get into my car.
We shared twelve years of happiness, you were my pride and joy.
You were my little shadow, my one and only boy.
Since you were so smart, house breaking was a breeze,
You could shake hands, roll over, do almost everything.
You'd lay there at the window, just waiting for me to get home,
Your companionship was remarkable, best I've ever known.
No matter where I was, you were always at my feet,
From the time we got up, until we went to sleep.
You loved my attention, loved chewing on bones,
Enjoyed playing with your toys, and barking at the unknown.

You loved me no matter, what the situation was,
You never asked for anything, never betrayed my trust.
You never made me feel unloved, or brought tears to my eyes,
Except for your sickness, and even then you tried -
To act like things were fine, and that you were feeling great,
But in reality, Boy, some things you just can't fake.
You were the first thing I saw each morning, the last face I saw at night,
Then came that dreaded day in September, it was our final goodbye.
When they had to put you to sleep, a part of me died,
But forever, you'll live, in this heart of mine.
I heard you bark when I came in the door, felt you in the bed at night,
So many days that followed, I thought I was losing my mind.

You could have really taught humans, about love and how to give,
Most have no clue what it means, or actually what it is.
You're now wagging in the sky, no doubt in Doggie Heaven,
Of all that I've been blessed with, you're truly one of my greatest
blessings.
You'll never be forgotten, well loved even past the end,
Makes me truly understand, a dog is your very best friend.

- Carol J. Hagan

So Much to Do

There are times in this life,
So much to do brings us strife.
Working each day,
Other things we delay.
Errands and shopping,
Cooking meals, we keep hopping.
Solving problems that cause a fuss,
At times, it is too much to keep up.
Cleaning the house and washing the car,
The hours in the day never go that far.
Cooking meals then doing dishes,
Even through this, we make daily wishes.
Feeding pets and planting flowers,
At the end of the day, trying to find time to take a shower.

All of the things that just have to be done,
Leave us so little time as we run and run.
So much to do that has to be done.
What time have we left for our family and fun?

Talks at the table before we start our day,
Finding out what others are facing, so we can diligently pray.
Knowing what "little things" to others mean so much,
Being certain that we are capable of others lives we can touch.
Favorite colors and songs, movies, desserts and what makes them giggle;
Knowing these things, we can give to them more than a little.
Wiping the tears and holding a hand,
Talking walks at dusk, just spending some time is grand.

All the things in life we just have to get done,
Be sure to do the ones that tomorrow aren't too late to be done.
Don't delay doing for what won't be there tomorrow.
Some of the things on this list, don't have time to borrow.
Choose what is important and what means the most,
Avoid the least on this list, being what you can boast.

Others are watching and waiting to see,
If we are living our lives for what we claim to be.
Especially for Christians who tell of God's love,
Be sure not to hinder those whom God is calling for from above.
The way we live and the things we "must" do,
Must be a true reflection of God that comes shining through.
If not then we hinder those He calls to Him,
We cannot be the reason others eternity is grim.
Choose ye today, to others what you will be.
Lead with your actions, everyone is looking - it could be me.

- Beverly S. Harless

Eighteen Years

One of the happiest moments, I've ever seen in my life,
Was May 19th, in 1995.
You entered life screaming, with tear filled eyes,
When place in my arms, you stopped, to my surprise.
You were such a tiny thing, so fragile and so weak,
Wasn't sure if I could do this, but you surely needed me.
The many countless hours, I'd hold you in my arms,
Playing with you, feeding you, protecting you from harm.
Teaching you how to walk, I'd hit the floor just in time,
To catch you when you fell, so you wouldn't get hurt or cry.
Potty training, bedtime stories, watching Barney 10,000 times,
The ABC's and 1-2-3's, and childhood nursery rhymes.
The first time you lost a tooth, the fairy came you know,
The priceless look upon your face, when Santa drank all the Coke.
Teaching you how to match your clothes, how to tie your shoes,
Playing at the park, and many days at the pool.
Building castles at the beach, only letting you play in the sand,
I was scared the waves would hurt you, but you didn't understand.
Your very first day of school, I was a nervous wreck,
All dressed up in brand new clothes, hair I'll never forget.
Homework, last minute projects, meetings like PTA,
Making sure you were doing good, and that you behaved.
Selling so much candy, I felt like the candy man,
If I could do it all over, I'm sure I'd sell again.
Tee ball, recitals, and all of those limo rides,
Skating, soccer, softball, made me proud you were mine.
Your very first bike, the Bratz, teletubbies, your first dog,
Taught you to say grace, and always believe in God.
To count your many blessings, others long for things you possess,
Treat people with respect, and always do your best.
The day you got your permit, then your after nines,
I was on pins and needles, as the minutes slipped by.
Sitting up to make sure, that you got home alright,
Eighteen years later, I still check on you each night.
Picking our your prom dress, making sure your night was great,
Your hair, makeup, shoes, everything in perfect place.
Been there through the good times, the anger, and attitudes,
Everything I've ever done, I did with love for you.
Today you turn 18, once you needed me so,
But in reality, I needed you, more than you know.

- Carol J. Hagan

Must I?

Must the words I say always be just right?
Must the deeds I do, to all bring delight?
Must the words I write be perfection in everyone's sight?
Or, must they just be done not in mine, but in the Lord's might?

Whether spoken or penned, if one thinks on them,
Or, it leads them to search for hours on end -
For the questions unleashed because of these things,
If they are searching for things of God, it makes Heaven sing.

If I delight many, or maybe just one,
With the deeds that I do - just to please God's Son,
The multitudes of voices to God doesn't matter -
As long as I please Jesus and He is the One that is flattered.

Should I discourage for things which I don't have a heart -
Simply because I am not willing to play that part?
I think not, I shall encourage instead,
I dare not discourage someone from going where God hath led.

Everything that I do may be filled with imperfection.
God can use these, too, to show His reflection.
It's the condition of the heart and our love for God's Son,
That will touch other hearts - even if it is only one.

- Beverly S. Harless

A So Called Dad

What do you think about an eighteen year old, yes one of those type of guys,
To avoid paying child support, they opt to give up their "rights".
That way they're not responsible, and can live their life care-free,
Not knowing and not caring, what or how she turns out to be.

While someone else is supporting, his biological little girl,
He travels to Hawaii and Paris, or anywhere else in the world.
He always drives a fancy car, he has money in the bank,
And the person that raised his child, not once has he ever said thanks.

He never attended her birthday parties, and she turned eighteen in May,
Never sent her a Christmas card, or a present on Christmas Day.
He's never bought any school clothes, not one single pair of shoes,
Never bought a pack of diapers, never made sure that she had food.

He's never been the Tooth Fairy, he's never played Santa Claus,
Never was the Easter Bunny, in fact he's never done anything at all.
He's never been to any school events, he's never heard her sing,
Never watched her play soccer, or any sports in little league.

He's never took her to a ball game, never heard her play in the band,
Never seen her playing at the park, or building castles in the sand.
He's never seen her swimming, never taught her how to dive,
Didn't offer a single dime, when she needed a car to drive.

He's never seen her sad or crying, never put a smile upon her face,
Never saw her on prom night, he's never met her date.
I'm sure by now you get the picture, he couldn't have cared less,
All he's ever really cared about, was caring for himself.

He won't attend her graduation, he won't walk her down the aisle,
He won't share the father-daughter dance, or see her in love smile.
He thinks he gained his freedom, when he signed away his little girl,
But, the child he never wanted, instantly became my whole world.

- Carol J. Hagan

A Long Hard Day

At the end of the day, most can say they are wiped out.
When answering a question, they don't mean to shout.
Problems arise throughout our day.
It seems, without them, there is no other way.
Things get hard, yet, we make it through.
Sometimes, we learn more than what we knew.
Muscles ache, and our heads feel like they're going to explode.
We take care of so much, it's often a heavy load.
Just when we think we are done, something else will arise.
Once in awhile, it turns out to be a nice surprise.
Stress levels are high, as we muddle through.
Sometimes, we just don't know what to do.

Starting my day with prayer and asking for help,
I know there's no way I can make it myself.
Each task that is started - another little prayer.
God gives me wisdom and courage - just because He cares.
Another little prayer as I re-enter my home.
Even at this, I can't handle, all there, on my own.
Crisis and problems - everyone seems to look to me,
Another little prayer, up to Heaven, has to be.
A long hard day is now history and in the past.
Peace and contentment, for all, a short time will last.
A long hard day fixed by prayers I did send.
Thank God for being my closest Friend.

- Beverly S. Harless

Dear Santa Clause

I was gonna make my yearly Christmas list, addressed to Santa Claus,
Ask you for all kinds of things, they I suddenly stopped and thought.
What do I really want, more like what do I really need,
Not one thing crossed my mind, compared to others I have everything.

Although it's not that fancy, I have a good home and it's clean,
I have a cozy king size bed, even high thread count sheets.
I have gas for my fireplace, and in the summer I have AC,
Come to think of it Santa, I can't think of a thing you need to bring to me.

I have food in my cabinets, and I'm not that hard to please,
It may not be caviar, but what I have works for me.
I have means of transportation, although it's far from being new,
I have plenty of clothes, I even wear New Balance shoes.

I've moved up in the world a bit, I now own one of those flat screens,
Still I'm thinking what in the world, could you actually bring to me.
I already have the best family, and friends that money can't buy,
I'm blessed beyond blessed, and theres so many reasons why.

So after all of this thinking, and pondering what I should ask,
I think I have the perfect request, that is if you're up for the task.
When you come calling at my house, during the night on Christmas Eve,
Whatever you think I wanted, please give it to someone that's in need.

Give my presents to that child, that feels left out and so alone,
Since their mom and dad left this earth, and now they're on their own.
Or drop mine off at a nursing home, and let them touch your suit,
I bet to some, if you showed up, they would still believe in you.

Send another gift of mine, to the Hope Station and then,
Make a grand entrance to the homeless, there's no telling how their life has been.
To the mother or dad that's forgotten, and so often feels betrayed,
Make this Christmas special, and visit them on Christmas Day.

One last request Dear Santa, that I sincerely as of you - if I may,
Send all the other gifts of mine to the troops, that protect the USA.
So tonight when the elves are busy, filling up you magical sleigh,
Please don't forget to leave me out, I'll let you get on your way.

- Carol J. Hagan

Let Your Light Shine

The places I go every day, are filled with darkness and dismay.
People needed a smiling face, as they try to make it through their
day.

Family close, but not lending a hand,
For someone to give compassion to them - is grand.
Chores and laundry that need to be done,
Many I see, really have no one.
Children have grown and have long left the nest,
While the parents get by - doing their best.
After visitors quit coming long ago,
Leaves the elderly wondering, where did they all go?
Watching the clock as the days pass by,
They spend many hours as they sit and cry.

In a world of darkness, we should let our light shine.
Sometimes, we are the only one who gives of our time.
Make them feel special - if only for a short while.
They go through so much, we often don't know their trials.
Have a cheerful voice - let that be what they hear from us.
Let meekness and love be what raises their spirits up.
Make a day better than it was before.
Light up their house as you knock on their door.
Give something to remember - until you return again.
All that is needed is to feel as though they have a friend.

The places I go - everyday, are fill with darkness and dismay.
Leave a Godly example allowing His love to light the way.

- Beverly S. Harless

Once an Adult, Twice a Child

I wake up and wonder, what this day will bring,
Will she remember my name, or remember anything.
Will she be sweet, kind and gentle, like the mother I always knew.
Or, will she be agitated, ill - or not even have a clue.
As to where she's now living or who I may be,
Am I still her daughter, or a fading memory.
Today I was her sister, tonight a childhood friend,
Yesterday I was her mother, and the cycle never ends.
Occasionally she remembers, and even calls me by my name,
Mostly I'm the "sweet girl" that visits her every day.
Often her son is her husband, her husband becomes her son.
Her grandchildren seem like strangers, memories destroyed one by one.
She sits in her recliner, talks to people that's not there,
I just nod in agreement, showing her that I care.
I listen to everything she says, holding on to every word,
Silently I'm crying, God why can't she be cured.

I've never seen her take a drink, never went to a bar,
Never lied or cheated, and loved my dad with all her heart.
She taught us about God, and to pray night and day,
Never judge a book by its cover, no matter what others say.
If you can't say something nice, by all means, keep quiet,
Never treat people, as if, "out of sight, out of mind".
Be kind and patient, always lend a helping hand,
For you never know the moment, you might be where they stand.
Be thankful that you have a job, do your best at work each day,
Others less fortunate would love to take your place.
Never go to bed angry, and walk away from useless fights,
The words you speak in anger, you might live with all your life.
Don't plant a cactus, expecting to produce a beautiful rose,
Be careful how you treat others, you'll reap whatever you sow.
She's been a chauffeur and a cook, my boo-boos she could mend,
A nurse, a maid, and advisor - my very, very best friend.

How could she go from a wise teacher, of life, in many ways,
Then become the fragile person, that she has become today.
She never won an Oscar or medal, for the great deeds she's done,
But, there's no doubt about it, she could have won every one.
Alzheimer's is a heartless disease, I detest its very name,
The heartache it brings to a family, is never ending pain.
They say, once and adult - twice a child, now I know what that means,
To watch life unfold before your eyes, and lose the meaning of everything.

- Carol J. Hagan

Other books published by the authors are:

One Night of Regrets: A Story of Restoration and Grace
by Beverly S. Harless

Made in the USA
Charleston, SC
30 June 2014